T0247865

DONE DEAL!

THE REAL ESTATE AGENT'S GUIDE TO MASTERING NEGOTIATIONS

SETH WEISSMAN AND **KATHARINE OATES**

Forefront
BOOKS

Published by Forefront Books.
Distributed by Simon & Schuster.

Library of Congress Control Number: 2023902665

Print ISBN: 978-1-63763-188-1
E-book ISBN: 978-1-63763-187-4

Cover Design by Bruce Gore, Gore Studios Inc.
Interior Design by Mary Susan Oleson, BLU Design Concepts

To Belishe Pompey,
without whose help and guidance
this book would not have been possible.

CONTENTS

ACKNOWLEDGMENTS

WE WOULD LIKE to thank the hundreds of agents who are too numerous to name who gave us ideas and feedback on this book. We would like to give special thanks to the following real estate brokers and agents who made special contributions to the final version of the book: Glennda Baker, Laura Rittenberg, Michele Velcheck, Stephen Walker, Catherine Newsome, Vinnie Lin, Nestor Rivera, Paula Henao, Robbie Roberts, Cindy Park, Teri Ehrlich, Nina Ehrlich, Karren Amidon, Kathryn Brown, Hugh Oates, Michelle Rios, Tiffany Byars, and DeAnn Golden.

ACKNOWLEDGMENTS

INTRODUCTION

AGENTS KNOW HOW important being a good negotiator is to their success. While there have been dozens of books written on negotiations, most of them are about face-to-face negotiations where the people negotiating are the only ones affected by the outcome. These books are great primers for negotiating things like buying a car. Unfortunately, they do not have much relevance to real estate negotiations, which, among other things, are almost never face-to-face and require agents to negotiate for their client rather than for themselves.

Now, for those hoping to learn the one quick and easy negotiation technique that will instantly transform you into a great negotiator, this book is probably not for you. While we would all welcome a magic negotiation pill, there is no cookie-cutter formula that will apply to all real estate negotiations. As we will explain throughout this book, there are simply too many variables that affect the outcome of each negotiation. Real estate negotiations are unpredictable at times, and no two are exactly alike. A negotiation strategy that helps a client get a great deal buying or selling a property one day, may unfortunately be an abject failure in a different transaction the next day.

Because negotiations to buy and sell houses are distinct from other types of negotiations, agents must build an equally distinct negotiation skill set tailored to the real estate brokerage industry. This book identifies and teaches agents these skills. They are the ones that we, as authors who love to negotiate, have seen used successfully in thousands of real estate transactions. We have also confirmed them in discussions with hundreds of successful real estate agents. Some of these skills may seem elementary when viewed in isolation. Collectively, however, they are the rock-solid, time-tested tools of a great real estate negotiator. Embracing these will not only make you a better negotiator, but if you continue to develop and practice them, they will also make you a much better agent.

In the absence of there being one magic technique to becoming a great real estate negotiator for buyers and sellers, there are two universal truths that agents should always remember:

TRUTH #1: Residential real estate negotiations take place in the context of the real estate market. In a balanced or shifting market, skilled agents can flex their negotiating muscles to craft amazing deals for their clients, regardless of whom they represent. In an extreme market, however, even the strongest negotiators will find it difficult to get their clients a great deal if the market favors the other party. Of course, the deal they get their clients by using great negotiation strategies may still truly be amazing when considering the market in which they are operating and when compared to results produced by agents without their skills.

For example, if you are representing the buyer in an extreme seller's market, it is unlikely you will get very far unless you quickly make an uncomplicated or "clean" offer at top dollar. Similarly, if you are representing a seller in an extreme buyer's market, you will be considered fortunate if you get even a single offer. In such cases, you will have few opportunities to negotiate terms, so learning approaches that will help you to capitalize on each of those opportunities becomes critical to your overall success as an agent.

TRUTH #2: For many buyers and sellers, negotiations to buy and sell houses are filled with more emotion than most other negotiations. Being aware of this fact and sympathetic to clients experiencing strong emotions—or at the least, mixed feelings about selling or buying a house—is one of the secrets to becoming a great real estate negotiator. This is particularly the case with sellers who have lived in a house long enough to have transformed it into a home. Our homes have special meaning to us, and the process of buying and selling them can generate strong emotions that sometimes interfere with what might otherwise be a rational, businesslike approach to a negotiation. Some agents attempt to remove emotion from their transactions and become unavoidably frustrated when they cannot do so completely. The agents who accept emotions as a given and learn to ride the emotional roller coasters our clients can occasionally take us on are better able to keep our clients focused on moving forward with the transaction.

The negotiating tools discussed in this book can

be used to the agent's advantage, regardless of who they may be representing in the transaction. All of the tools are purposeful and, if practiced, will help agents master the art of real estate negotiations.

Chapter 1

WHAT MAKES RESIDENTIAL REAL ESTATE NEGOTIATIONS SO DIFFICULT?

WHAT MAKES NEGOTIATING over the purchase and sale of a house so difficult? The answer is plenty. First, in residential real estate negotiations, there tend to be a lot of cooks in the proverbial kitchen. If there are two buyers, two sellers, and an agent on each side of a transaction, then that is six people who are each playing various roles in the negotiation. And do not forget the well-intentioned friends and extended family members of the parties who are offering their opinions on the merits of the transaction and whether the buyer and seller are getting a good or bad deal. Add in a dollop of emotion and a tablespoon of stress, and you have a recipe for a potentially disastrous negotiation. While the more the merrier is fine at a Thanksgiving dinner (it is, right?), it tends to make negotiating far more complicated as each person contributes their unique perspective to the negotiation.

Second, real estate negotiations are particularly difficult because they involve people with wide ranges of sophistication and expertise as negotiators. Many of them do not buy or sell houses very often, which complicates matters further. As a result, without the agent's help, people frequently have unrealistic expectations, make mistakes, and lose focus on important issues. Part of an agent's job is to protect their clients from themselves, which is a balancing act that takes finesse and patience.

From the agent's perspective, it is hard to say whether it is worse to have a client who admittedly does not know much about negotiations or a client who regularly negotiates other types of deals and therefore fancies herself an expert on all negotiations, including real estate negotiations. Most of the agents we spoke with said that they prefer the former because those without expertise can at least be guided in the right direction. The so-called experts are usually the ones who are the most stubborn and the quickest to blame the agent if things do not go well.

Third, for most people, a house is their single largest asset, which means that mistakes can have a long-term, negative impact. Having real money at risk makes buying and selling homes a scary proposition whether you are just starting out, growing a family, or preparing for retirement. Even seasoned agents tell us that they experience increased anxiety and approach negotiations differently when they buy or sell their own personal homes. This doesn't happen because they suddenly forget how to evaluate properties or how to negotiate contracts. It happens, at least in part, because they could be facing financial losses if they make poor decisions. Agents who regularly talk to their clients and acknowledge that being somewhat fearful is completely normal are more likely to be viewed as empathetic by their clients. This can help build a bond and greater trust.

Fourth, houses are also homes. The desire to own a home remains the primary American dream and affects how people see themselves. Desiring a home that will enhance one's self-image can be a powerful motivator for a buyer. For many of us, our homes are a reflection of who we are as people: our tastes, financial status, personality, and lifestyle.

When a person sells their home, they are inviting strangers into their personal space and can get their feelings hurt when that space is judged negatively. Sellers who have been prepared by their agents in advance of buyers seeing the house know that some criticism is likely a part of the real estate negotiation game and are usually less emotional and more able to let such criticism roll off their backs.

The bottom line is that real estate transactions can be emotionally charged. Moves are frequently precipitated by major life changes such as death, divorce, marriage, the birth of a child, or a job change. Experiencing any of these life-altering events elicits emotional responses that range from depression to excitement. The degree to which buyers and sellers respond emotionally in negotiations over the purchase and sale of their house is often exaggerated by these situational stressors and can have a huge impact on the outcome.

Over the course of a negotiation to buy or sell real estate, buyers and sellers can often express a wide range of emotions, including impatience, indecision, frustration, anger, relief, and excitement. These emotions can affect rational decision- making and at times lead to unpredictable results. These can include buyers and sellers unexpectedly backing out of a deal midstream or contracts falling apart over who will pay for a repair costing a few hundred dollars. Again, agents who can be empathetic to these swings in emotions, but constantly remind their clients of the many rational reasons why they are buying or selling a house, usually get more deals across the finish line.

Of course, some people have no attachment to real estate other than an economic one. To investors or others who regularly relocate for work, a house is often just a commodity. Part of an agent's job is to learn who the buyers and sellers are and what motivates them. To do that, the agent must ask questions and look for clues. If you pay attention to what matters to your client, it becomes much easier to determine how best to communicate with them.

Fifth, unlike most every other type of negotiation, the negotiation to buy or sell a house usually involves complete strangers who almost never have face-to-face meetings. Instead, deals are made through agent intermediaries who speak for their clients. Goodwill is often created when parties meet in person to negotiate a business deal. When you look somebody in the eye, observe their body language, and hear the tone of their voice, you are able to make first-person assessments about their credibility and sense of fair play.

When parties do not meet face-to-face and do not even speak to one another directly, it becomes very challenging to know who they are as people. Therefore, parties to a negotiation to buy and sell a house are often quicker to mistrust and misinterpret the intentions of the other party. Two key roles of the agent, as discussed later in this book, are to build rapport with the other agent and to assure that agent (and hopefully her client) that you and your client are reasonable and trustworthy.

With these types of difficulties, it is often a wonder that any real estate negotiations end up with the parties signing a contract, eventually smiling and laughing at a closing table, and privately commenting how much nicer the other party is than what they may have initially thought. Yet, somehow, through it all, the need or desire to buy and sell this special asset called a home manages to prevail. When agents understand the broader context in which real estate negotiations take place, the process tends to go far more smoothly.

Chapter 2

UNDERSTAND YOUR CLIENT AND REMEMBER THAT IT'S THEIR NEGOTIATION

DETERMINING YOUR CLIENTS' true motivations and what issues are most important to them is a critical part of being able to negotiate both with a client and on their behalf. This is not always easy to do. Some people are more private than others, so asking personal questions can at times be awkward. Second, your client might not always know what they want. They sometimes need help figuring out their options in any given real estate market. When representing couples, there are also times when they disagree with one another about what they want. Finally, it can sometimes be difficult to remember that it is your client's negotiation, not yours. While your expertise matters, your personal preferences should not—unless the choices your clients are making may hurt them financially.

At the beginning of any client relationship, the agent should emphasize the importance of being open and honest. You might start by saying something like "The most important thing that I can do for you is to ensure that your [sale/purchase] achieves what matters most to you. I cannot do that unless we are able to speak candidly throughout the process about your goals and preferences. Sometimes, that means that we have to discuss personal topics. Of course, you are always welcome to tell me you'd prefer not to discuss a particular issue. However, the more you are open and honest with me, the more I will be able to help you achieve your goals."

It is amazing how much easier it becomes to ask difficult questions when you've set the expectation that doing so is necessary. Naturally, you will still need to be tactful about how you ask those questions and give context to those that are personal. For example, if your seller is going through a divorce, you will need to ask questions about the legal status of the relationship to make sure the contract reflects the required approvals needed to sell the property.

And again, there are times when the client does not fully know what they want. In particular, buyers will sometimes tell you that they are interested in buying one type of house only to be continually attracted to and ultimately buy a completely different type of house. Some buyers really do not know what they want or have conflicts between their hearts, their heads, and their wallets when it comes to the houses and neighborhoods in which they want to live.

As we will discuss in greater detail later in this book, some clients do not have realistic expectations or any expectations, for that matter. Instead, they rely on you to help them develop reasonable expectations. At other times, the client has expectations that are out of line with the realities of the market. This is the buyer client who wants a huge price reduction on houses in an extreme seller's market, or the seller who does not want to spend money to get the house ready to list in a buyer's market. If the agent cannot convince the client to have realistic expectations consistent with the market, it may be better to let the client find a different agent.

When your buyers will be financing their purchase, it is always a good idea to get them prequalified prior to showing them homes. In doing so, you don't waste time showing them houses they cannot afford. You can then send them copies of the listings in their target area that fit within their budget, even those where the configuration isn't precisely what they said they wanted. Sometimes, people need to see with their own eyes what their money can buy. Of course, the things that matter most to your client can also change after you have gone under contract as well, so it is important to continually touch base.

Representing couples can also be challenging because they do not always want the same things. Great agent negotiators quickly try to figure out how couples make decisions and who the decision maker is on differing aspects of the transaction. Is there a dominant partner who rules the roost, or is it more of a collaborative effort? The answer is not always obvious, and since every couple is different, agents can figure it out only by watching and observing.

Agents tell us that couples argue with each other in front of them with surprising frequency. The agent has a few choices when this occurs. She can tell her clients that she is going to step outside to take a call while they discuss it to give them space. She might also try to suggest solutions that might appeal to both parties. If those options do not work, then it is probably a good idea to take a break and regroup once they have reached a resolution.

Whether your clients are individuals, couples, or some other grouping, an agent must learn what their client's preferences are without steering them. To do this, begin with very open-ended questions and avoid adding opinionated statements to your questions and conversations. So, for example, if you and your buyer are driving through a neighborhood with older homes, you wouldn't say, "The homes in this neighborhood are dated, do you really want to see them?" Instead, simply ask, "What do you think about the homes in this neighborhood?" There are two reasons for this. First, you want to get your client's true feelings without your influence. Second, there are some questions that can result in potential fair housing issues.

Understandably, clients often ask for their agent's opinion as experts in the field. That is part of the value an agent brings to their client. The key to answering such questions is to present facts objectively. So, for example, if your client asks you what your thoughts are about the homes in that same older neighborhood, you could answer the question with something like the following: "Most of the homes in this neighborhood were built in the 1930s. Many people find older homes quite charming, but they often need to be updated and may not meet current building codes. Of course, a good home inspector can help identify if there are problems, so if there is a home in this neighborhood that interests you, let's take a look."

One of the harder lessons for agents to learn is that it is your client's negotiation, not yours. There are many times when agents watch their buyer clients pay more for their homes than they would personally pay or watch their seller clients sell their homes for less than they would personally accept. While this can be frustrating at times to watch, the lesson should always be that if your client is happy with the outcome, you should also be happy, even if you think you might have been able to press for a better deal.

What agents should also remember is that while they likely could have pushed for more concessions had they been the buyer or seller, every request or demand for a concession involves a risk-benefit analysis. There is a risk associated with every request for concession, which usually is the possibility of the deal falling apart. Many buyers and sellers analyze that risk more cautiously than agents. Clearly present the facts, including risks and likelihood of success. Then allow your client to make the ultimate choice and respect their decision.

Sometimes, an agent will push for concessions beyond what the client wanted or asked for, thinking that the client will be extra happy with the result. If the strategy works, the agent is the hero. However, if the strategy does not work, and the transaction falls apart, the agent is the scape goat and may end up getting fired. This underscores the value of knowing what your client wants and stopping when those goals are achieved.

The bottom line is that when working with clients, there is no substitute for (1) constantly asking questions and observing what makes them tick and (2) confirming every step in the negotiation process to make sure that the statements you make reflect their goals and wishes. Without doing both of those things, the agent is negotiating in the dark. In this regard, some of the most common phrases used by agents in negotiations should be "Let me check with the buyers" or "Let me check with the sellers." Your judgment should never be substituted for their decision-making.

Chapter 3

SETTING REALISTIC EXPECTATIONS

BUYERS AND SELLERS often have unrealistic expectations about the value of particular properties. Sellers inevitably think their homes are worth more than they really are. Buyers think that the properties they are considering buying should be worth less. Not surprisingly, expectations sometimes follow preferences and wallets instead of the market. Theoretically, expectations should begin to align with the market when a party's initial efforts to buy at a discounted price or sell at an inflated price are unfulfilled. In reality, however, it is not always that simple.

Setting a client's expectations is a delicate matter and not always easy to do. Some agents will encourage sellers to go visit listings that will compete with their own listing to see exactly where their home stacks up in the marketplace. Others prefer to allow their buyers and sellers to be rebuffed in the market for some period of time instead of having honest conversations with them. Letting a client learn by having their efforts to buy or sell a home fail does the client a disservice.

If a seller prices a home too high above market, for example, the home will likely sit on the market and become stale. Such listings tend to sell for even less than they would have had they been priced correctly at the outset. Similarly, buyers could lose out on the home of their dreams if their agent waits too long to correct misguided assumptions about what their money can buy.

One of the hardest times to set expectations is in a changing market because shifts in client expectations tend to be slower than the shifts in the market. In an extreme seller's market, a seller may get substantially more money for their home than a neighbor with an identical house would after the market has begun to slow. Explaining to a client that the market has turned and that they now have to accept less money than they would have been able to get only a few months before is always challenging.

The best way to help set realistic expectations is with

data. You can show your client information about pricing in the area and time on market. You can show them historical data and overall market trends in the general area and then in the specific neighborhood. Sometimes, seeing it on paper helps. This is also a neutral way that the agent can explain the realities of the situation without insulting their client.

One key is to be very intentional about the data you share. It isn't enough for an agent to show an unrealistic client only the average price for comparable homes. Instead, agents must first determine how the client has reached an incorrect conclusion about home values. Was it simply wishful thinking, or have they seen or heard something that skewed their perception? Once the source is known, an agent can determine what solution will work best to help reset the client's expectations. Consider the following examples of data that can be used to explain actual market conditions and to emphasize the risk of proceeding based on faulty assumptions:

1. **Average price fluctuations over the last six months in a particular neighborhood compared to price fluctuations in the county, the state, and the national real estate market.** This is useful when you

are trying to show a client that what they are hearing on the news or on social media isn't necessarily the reality in their specific area.

2. **Sale-to-list ratio for prices in a particular neighborhood or area.** This is useful to show a buyer during a discussion about how much to offer. If correctly priced homes in a particular area sell for 98 percent of list price, for example, then a 90 percent offer is unrealistic.

3. **List price to fair market value ratio in relation to time on market.** This is useful to show unrealistic sellers that houses that are listed too high sit on the market longer and risk becoming stale.

4. **Sale-to-list ratios for prices in relation to time on market.** This is useful to discuss with sellers to show them that homes that are listed too high ultimately sell for less than correctly priced homes.

If your client doesn't respond well to data and numbers, another way to help them adjust their expectations is to show them photographs of actual listings that have sold or take them on a tour of actively listed homes at a similar price point. This can work for buyers and sellers. A seller who wants to list her house for $800,000 might need to see that other homes listed at $800,000 have more bedrooms or are fully renovated before they can understand why a buyer might not pay that price for their home. Similarly, a buyer who thinks the price she is willing to pay will buy more house than is realistic might not understand until you show them houses in the price point. After all, seeing is generally believing. That might just be the reality check that your client needs. Of course, there is always the client that sees their dated, poorly maintained, or functionally obsolete home as equivalent to an updated, well-maintained, and well-laid-out house. In this case the agent has to decide if it is worth spending the time trying to sell a house that may sit unsold on the market.

What happens when the party on the other side of the transaction has unrealistic expectations? This is certainly more difficult to change. When a buyer makes a low offer, it is usually for one of three reasons:

1. The buyer's agent is inexperienced and did not properly set the buyer's expectations.

2. The buyer is not listening to her agent.

3. The buyer is just testing the seller to see how she might respond to a low offer.

A seller's agent cannot automatically assume that it is one reason over the other. When a lowball offer is made, some agents advise their clients not to respond. Others will indignantly announce that their client was insulted by the offer. Is this the right approach? In most cases, the answer is no. When the response to the low offer is anger or silence, it puts off many buyers, and they may go looking elsewhere for a house. In an extreme seller's market, of course, it is easy to blow off such offers knowing that there are other buyers likely champing at the bit to buy the property. Still, you never know if you will be showing a buyer that agent's listing next week. How you treat them today might very well impact how they treat you tomorrow.

When the low offer arrives, the smart agent will tell their seller to make a nominal reduction in her price, such as $500, and return it to the buyer. This politely tells the buyer that her offer is not in the ballpark but leaves the door open to further negotiations. If the buyer was testing the seller, then the seller just passed the test. If the buyer was unrealistic or uninformed, this leaves the door open for more discussions and enlightenment.

Another way to help reshape unrealistic expectations

on the other side of the transaction is to enlist the help of the other agent. This can be particularly challenging if the other agent is the one fueling their client's expectations, but it is doable if you remain calm. Telling somebody that their beliefs or opinions are unrealistic or arguing with them angers people more than persuades them. If, on the other hand, you remain polite and understanding, then they will likely be more cooperative as well.

One great way to work around an obstacle without becoming combative is to align yourself with the other agent. Use phrases like "I'd love to make this transaction happen for you and your client." People respond well when they believe you are on their side. It is amazing how flexible people become when they feel like you are working together to reach the same goal. Consider the following example in this interaction:

Buyer's agent: "My buyer thinks the home is worth $450,000, and frankly, I agree."

Seller's agent: "There is nothing I'd like more than for your client to get this house. The seller knows that 123 Cherry Street sold for $480,000, so accepting the buyer's offer just doesn't make sense to her. I'd welcome any information you can give me to share with the seller. I'll present it to the seller immediately and see if it will help get a deal done here."

Notice how the seller's agent gave the seller's position credibility and defended it while simultaneously aligning herself with the buyer's agent. This subtle move from, "you're wrong because . . ." to "help give me the information I need to convince my seller . . ." is nonconfrontational and puts the burden on the buyer's agent to come up with something that will help get the parties under contract. As a result, the buyer's agent will hopefully become far more flexible and open-minded about the seller's position.

One of the great challenges in the real estate brokerage industry is the wide disparity in agent expertise. Many agents are amazingly smart and talented and have great negotiation skills. Others, not so much. As a result, some of the offers and counteroffers agents receive are way out of line with the market. Rather than becoming frustrated with what can be the unexpected twists and turns in the negotiation process, it is best to be patient and remember the job we have been hired to do by our clients. Agents with little negotiation expertise make many mistakes that ultimately benefit the other agent and their client. Keeping the door open in these situations by trying to be helpful allows the experienced agent to get their client the best results. Burning bridges is rarely the right way to proceed.

Next, it must be remembered that ultimately, the price at which the seller will sell, and the buyer will buy, does not always have to be be rational. After all, it is what a buyer will pay and the seller will accept that determines the sales price of a property. If you are representing the seller, there is nothing wrong in saying that regardless of the data, if the buyer wants to buy the house today, this is the price the buyer will need to pay. The same can also be said in reverse to the seller, that this is the price this particular buyer is willing to pay today to purchase a property. If a buyer wants to buy badly enough, and if a seller wants to sell badly enough, the true fair market value of the property often goes right out the window.

Another challenge that agents have is that some of their clients either are, or at least think they are, great negotiators. It can sometimes be hard to establish your own credibility as a competent negotiator when your client believes they are the master of the craft. Rather than trying to prove your negotiating bona fides to your client, it usually makes the most sense to follow your client's lead in such situations. After all, the client is the one who will ultimately be buying or selling a house. But, of course, you also do not want to waste a lot of time if your client makes mistakes because she does not understand the market.

A compromise that usually works is to acknowledge your client's negotiating expertise but to explain to your client that what you bring to the table is knowledge of the market. The struggle is to convince your client that it is the combination of the two that makes for a successful outcome in buying or selling a house. Here is one possible script to do that:

> "Mr. Jones, you obviously have a lot of expertise as a negotiator, and I am glad to follow your lead in negotiating the best deal possible. Where I can be of value is to help you better understand the real estate market in which you will be negotiating and what the other agent is likely thinking and advising her client. In that way, we can work together to get you the best deal possible."

Regardless of your client's negotiation skills, working with them to develop a realistic expectation of the market will help everyone avoid wasting time. How does one do that? On the sales side, clients who are expert negotiators still need to know (and constantly be reminded) of the following:

1. What have similar homes sold for in the past and what are they selling for now? (These are your "comps.")

2. On average, how long are homes staying on the market?

3. How long could the listed home stay on the market?

4. On average, at what percentage above or below the list price are homes selling for?

5. At what percentage of the list price should the listed property sell for?

6. What updates/improvements will increase the value of the home and make sense to do?

7. How much, if anything, does the seller contribute to buyer's closing costs to help get the transaction closed?

8. How long is a normal due diligence period?

9. How long of a financing and appraisal contingency should there be?

10. How much earnest money is typical?

Now, obviously, the agent will not likely have answers to all of these questions. But the agent will have far better information than the homeowner (even one who is a great negotiator). The more the seller understands the process and the issues that are negotiated, the more the seller will feel in control of the transaction.

On the buyer's side, buyer agents need to give the same type of information to their buyer clients. The point is that even great negotiators need to have a context to negotiate—and the agent is the one who provides that. Without that context, the buyer may end up making a ridiculous offer way out of line with the realities of the market and just make the agent look foolish.

Setting realistic expectations also involves educating the buyer on what she can expect to buy for the money she has available to spend. Expectations can change as a person goes through the home buying or home selling process. But negotiating for a price at which the buyer cannot offer to buy, and the seller cannot afford to sell, makes little sense.

Chapter 4

KNOW THE VALUE OF PROPERTIES YOU ARE NEGOTIATING TO BUY OR SELL

You CAN NEVER negotiate to buy or sell something at a great price if you do not already know its true value. Imagine walking onto a used car lot and trying to negotiate the purchase of a car where the only information you had was a price given to you by the salesperson. Are you going to do as well as a buyer who researches the price at which other similar cars have sold? The answer, of course, is no. Without knowing whether the used car dealer will negotiate off of the stated price, and by how much, you are likely going to overpay. The same principle applies to buyers negotiating to buy or sell real estate for their clients.

Determining the true value of real estate requires the agent to do thorough research on comparable home sales or what some agents call a Comparable Market Analysis (CMA). Of course, there are comps and then there are meaningful comps. To be of any real use, the comp must be close to the subject property, it must have sold recently (within the last three to six months, depending on the market), and it must be a truly similar property. When determining what homes are relevant comps, agents should focus on the unique features of each property in determining whether it should command a higher or lower price. Questions like the following should always be asked:

- Is the house in a good location?

- Has the house been updated?

- Has it been well maintained?

- Does it have a good floor plan?

- Is it larger or smaller than other homes in the community?

- Is the lot larger or smaller?

- Does the property offer privacy?

- Is the landscaping attractive?

- Does the house have special features like a pool or a particularly nice view?

- Is the property in a good school district?

It's these details that can be used to distinguish one property from the next and which a good negotiator can use to create a thorough comparative market analysis, and ultimately, to get a better deal.

A CMA, like an appraisal, is a look backward. While looking backward is a fundamental part of successful real estate negotiations and should not be discounted, agents should remember the importance of also looking forward at where the market is heading.

Agents must therefore evaluate the overall housing trends affecting the neighborhood and the broader community in which the subject property is located. This kind of information is generally not found in a book or a government office. Instead, agents must learn to ask the right questions and to trust their judgment regarding the answers. So what are the "right" questions? That answer might differ from state to state and area to area, but generally speaking, an evaluation of the neighborhood and broader community requires asking questions like these:

- Are owners investing in their homes?

- Are neighborhood homes mostly owner-occupied or rented?

- Is the neighborhood aging well?

- Are local shops and services getting better or worse?

- Are there regional changes that are affecting values in the community?

- Are property taxes usually high?

A neighborhood can be well kept with nice homes, but if the trends for the broader community are negative, it will eventually bring down the value of the properties in even the nicest of neighborhoods. Similarly, some listing agents get so accustomed to seeing values in a neighborhood at a particular level that they may overlook the broader trends impacting home values in the area. In doing so, they are doing a true disservice to their clients.

There is a suburban neighborhood near Atlanta, Georgia, that is a great example of this. When the homes in this particular neighborhood were originally built, they were naturally considered less desirable than their in-town counterparts because they were far away from employment and entertainment centers. Thirty years of urban sprawl later, as commercial development has pushed beyond the city limits and as new homes have been built farther and farther away from the city hub, this neighborhood that was once deemed "far out" is now considered "close in" to the city. Homes in the neighborhood have aged well and most are on larger private lots than the lots in newer communities. Most importantly, prices in other similarly situated neighborhoods have increased significantly.

One might expect that the home values in this neighborhood have skyrocketed, and while they have certainly increased over the last three decades, the growth has been much slower than in surrounding neighborhoods. What caused this phenomenon? It is impossible to say for sure; however, it is interesting that the same small group of agents has largely been listing the homes in the neighborhood for many years. They advertised themselves as neighborhood experts, so when advising their clients about home prices, perhaps they believed that looking at broader area trends was unnecessary. Had they noticed the larger trends quietly reshaping other nearby neighborhoods, they most certainly would have sought higher asking prices for the homes they were trying to sell.

Instead, these agents advised their sellers to list at safe

prices knowing that the homes would sell quickly. They did not push prices. A couple of agents who had familiarity with the broader trends encouraged their clients to buy homes in the neighborhood knowing that prices in other similar neighborhoods had already risen. Prices eventually began to rise sharply, and these savvy agents were rewarded with lifelong clients who appreciated their expertise. Did they negotiate a great deal for their clients? Not necessarily in a traditional sense, but their actions in studying the true value of homes in the broader community made the difference in terms of getting their clients great deals.

What caused the sudden run-up in prices? As an agent explained, "One day, a particularly desirable property in the neighborhood went on the market. Bidders realized it was a special house and offered more than twice what the old-time established listing agents said it was worth. This set off a flurry of home sales at substantially higher prices." How did the old-time listing agents miss the trend? According to the agent, they focused on what was safe and known rather than what was achievable and ignored the broader trends affecting the neighborhood.

Finally, an agent must expand their research from

the micro local area trends to the macro national trends. Interest rates, the economy, the availability of housing, demographics (in terms of the ages and numbers) of home-buyers, and more all affect the ultimate price of housing. The point is that knowing the true value of something is what always allows a great negotiator to get the best deal for their clients. True value can be obtained only through research and study.

Price negotiations are often the most important part of a real estate transaction. They begin before the home even hits the market and often continue throughout a transaction until the deal officially closes. An agent who has done their homework can determine if a property is overpriced, a bargain, or somewhere in between. With this knowledge, even an inexperienced agent can gain an advantage in a negotiation to buy or sell a house.

Chapter 5

ASK LOTS OF QUESTIONS AND LISTEN

A GREAT NEGOTIATOR learns to connect with the people with whom they are negotiating and to ask lots of questions. One never knows how the information gleaned from asking questions is going to help you. But, as anyone who has ever negotiated will tell you, the more information you have, the better able you are to tailor an offer that will meet the needs of the other party.

What kinds of questions might a buyer agent ask the other agent? Set forth below are some of the more common questions listing agents get asked. Of course, not all of these questions should be asked at the same time:

1. Why are the sellers moving?

2. Do the sellers have any special timing needs?

3. Do the sellers have any hot button issues to avoid in making an offer?

4. Is there anything else my buyers should know about the sellers or the property before they make an offer?

5. What would a perfect offer look like to the seller?

6. Have there been previous offers on the property that fell through? If so, why?

7. When was the house built?

8. How long have the sellers lived in the house?

9. Are the sellers living in the house now?

10. Is the property served by sewer or septic?

11. How large is the property?

12. Do you have a survey of the property?

13. What is the school district for the property?

14. How large is the house?

15. Is the property served by public water?

16. Will the buyer become a member of any homeowners association?

17. Has the house been recently inspected by a home inspector? If so, did the inspector discover anything of concern?

18. Are there any issues with the neighbors?

19. Are there any encroachments onto the property?

20. Are there any easements over the property except for normal utility easements?

21. Do any improvements on the property encroach onto the neighbor's property?

22. Has there ever been any flooding on the property?

23. Has the seller filled out a property disclosure statement? If not, why not?

Now the answers to some of these questions may already be in the multiple listing service, in a seller's property disclosure statement, or in easily accessible public records. While there is no need to add questions multiple times, if there are any questions where you remain unsure of the correct answer, you should always ask additional questions. Ideally, the answers that are important to your clients should be included in the contract as seller warranties.

Negotiators seeking the maximum amount of information should start by asking broad general questions that lead to general discussions and possible follow-up questions rather than specific questions that illicit short answers. While both are important, the broader questions tend to yield more surprises if they lead in an unexpected direction. Listing agents are also encouraged to ask questions, although to avoid fair housing issues, most of these are limited to the financial ability of the buyer to purchase the property.

While every good negotiator wants to learn as much as they can about the other agent and their client, most great negotiators believe it is a mistake to reveal too much about themselves and their clients.

While this sounds great, it is not always the best advice. What is a better suggestion is to be strategic and deliberate in what you reveal about your client. Rule #1 should always be never reveal anything that might harm the negotiating position of your client. Sadly, this rule is often violated by well-meaning agents who do not even realize that they are saying things that could harm their client's negotiating position.

So, what is okay to reveal and not reveal? Let's look at the following statements and answer yes or no regarding whether it should be revealed.

1. My clients are getting a divorce. NO
2. The breadwinner in the family lost her job, and they need to sell. NO

3. There's a prison planned nearby, and my clients don't want to live near it. NO

4. The husband got transferred to a different city, and they need to move quickly for him to start his job. NO

5. My clients have an unrealistically high sense of what their property is worth. NO

6. The property is listed for $X, but I think the sellers will likely take $Y for the house. NO

7. My clients got a steal when they bought his house, and now they want to cash out. NO

8. The house needs a lot of repairs, and the sellers decided to move now rather than do all of that work. NO

9. The wife has cancer, and they want to live closer to the hospital. NO.

10. The owner is a widow and is unfamiliar with the world of real estate. NO

11. The sellers are worried that we are heading into a recession and that prices might fall. NO

Each of these statements should not be made because they either reveal some weakness about the seller, indicates a need to sell quickly, or otherwise forms the seller's negotiating position. Now, let's look at some statements that might be fine to reveal.

1. The sellers do not have to sell. YES

2. The sellers have said they will sell only if they get their price. YES

3. The sellers raised their family in this house, and it will be hard for them to leave. YES

4. There is a lot of interest in the property. YES

5. The sellers are looking to downsize. YES

By contrast, these statements are either neutral or reveal information that tends to confirm that the sellers will not be pushovers. While a great negotiator will not reveal information that is damaging to their client's position, building rapport with the other agent is helpful to getting a deal done. Agents are therefore encouraged to talk with the other agent, but limit yourself to innocuous subjects like the weather, food, and other topics that will not likely get you in trouble.

As one agent friend explained, whenever she is uncertain whether or not to reveal something, she pretends the client is standing behind her and asks herself whether or not they would be happy with the revelation.

Chapter 6

LEARN TO BE HYPER-OBSERVANT

BEING EXTRA OBSERVANT is one of the secrets of great negotiators. Most of us spend so much time thinking about what we are going to say next, we miss the nuances in what we are seeing and hearing around us. Being observant does not just mean paying a little more attention. It really means trying to be hyper-observant in hopes of learning more about a property, the parties, and the other agent with whom we are negotiating.

For a buyer's agent, being observant requires a high level of diligence when you walk through a house. Most buyers walk through the properties they are buying and completely miss sheetrock cracks, settlement, dents and scratches in the floor and walls, and all manner of things they will regret not noticing a week or two after moving into the house. Why is that? In the excitement of a possible purchase, our brains focus on the big picture of the house and our eyes completely miss the details. In other words, they see what they want to see and what they expect to see.

There was a famous experiment where people were asked to watch a video of several people bouncing a ball and were asked to count the total number of times the ball was bounced. During the video, a man dressed in a gorilla suit walked into the middle of the scene, pounded on his chest several times, and then walked off the screen. Afterward, the volunteers who were watching the video in the experiment were asked if they saw the gorilla. Most laughed and assumed that the person asking the question was joking because they completely missed what had literally been right in front of their eyes. They were shocked when the video was replayed and they saw the gorilla that they originally missed. The point of the experiment is that we can concentrate on one thing so carefully (in that case, the bouncing balls), that we literally become blind to other things right in front of our eyes.

The gorillas that most homebuyers tend to miss are

all of the little flaws and defects in a house. The agent can help the buyer identify these things.

By being hyper-observant, the agent can also gain insights that might be helpful in the negotiation. Questions that should run through the mind of an observant agent include the following:

1. Is the furniture new or old? (A sign of the financial condition of the seller)

2. What kind of condition are the floors in? (A sign of the financial condition of the seller and future maintenance for the buyer)

3. Does the house need painting? (A sign of the financial condition of the seller and future maintenance for the buyer)

4. Is furniture missing from rooms or clothing missing from closets? (A sign of a divorce)

5. Are there sheetrock cracks or settlement? (If major, a sign of potential structural issues)

6. Has the house been professionally staged? (A sign of a seller trying to maximize value)

7. Does the house or its lowest level smell musty? (A sign of possible moisture)

8. Is the house unusually cold? (Sometimes low temperatures help mask pet odors)

9. Does the house smell perfumed? (Often used to mask pet odors)

10. Is there furniture in odd places? (Often a question of whether the furniture is hiding something behind it)

11. Is there a room dehumidifier anywhere? (Often a sign of moisture)

12. Are there rugs in unusual places? (Often a question of what is under the rug)

13. Are there water stains on any walls or ceilings? (A sign of leaks or water penetration)

14. Do exterior elevations slope toward or away from the house? (Could be evidence of moisture)

15. Is there evidence of wood rot?(Obviously, a sign of a poorly maintained home)

Now, obviously, your role is not to be the home inspector. But sizing up the general condition of the house can help your buyer determine its value, whether significant repairs and improvements will be needed, and the possible motivation of the seller in selling. It is also okay to point out areas of concern to the buyer or home inspector so that further professional evaluations can be undertaken.

Where being hyper-observant can also be beneficial is in your conversations with the other agent. It can be very enlightening in these conversations if you can detach yourself enough to ask the following types of questions objectively of the listing agent:

1. Is she working hard to be helpful and professional and to get the house sold?

2. Does she seem motivated to sell, or is she going through the motions?

3. Is she answering questions honestly and completely?

4. Is there anything she is de-emphasizing about the property?

5. How is she trying to sell the property? What is she emphasizing?

6. Is she indicating flexibility on the part of the seller?

Again, her demeanor and her answers can tell you a lot about whether she thinks the property will sell to your buyer and at what price. Asking questions objectively and being hyper-observant is also important when you are representing a seller. Not only will it help you price the house accurately, but it will also help you understand what motivates your client. Equally important, being intentional about what you ask the buyer's agent and focusing on what the buyer's agent says about the buyer might give you insight about how to approach the negotiation.

Chapter 7

LEARN THE VALUE OF FRIENDLINESS

AN ENGLISH PROVERB holds that "you catch more flies with honey than with vinegar," and that is certainly true when it comes to real estate transactions. Being friendly is the one trait that universally seems to improve an agent's chances for a successful outcome in a negotiation.

When you perceive the person with whom you are negotiating as friendly, you are more inclined to agree with them, make concessions, and to do favors for them. This is a huge plus in a negotiation. The opposite also appears to be the case. If you are negotiating with a person who is unfriendly, you are less inclined to agree with them, to make concessions, or to do favors for them. Being friendly is more than having a pleasant disposition. It also means being credible, helpful, and professional in all of your interactions with the other agent, and it means trying to establish a good rapport with them that will last through many transactions.

A good negotiator tries to make the life of the other agent as easy as possible. If the other agent did not receive an email, you immediately send it again. If there are showing instructions in the listing, follow them. If you make a showing appointment, do everything you can to keep it. If the other agent wants feedback on the property, you gladly give thoughtful feedback. If the parties verbally agree on the terms of a counteroffer, you kindly offer to reduce it to writing. If you represent the seller and the other agent needs information that you have or can get, you quickly provide it.

Being friendly also means being credible and professional. No one likes to work with an agent who can't be trusted or speaks in half-truths. Being credible and professional means you do what you say you are going to do and acknowledge whatever the realities are of the transaction.

If the house is in terrible condition and needs a tremendous amount of work, the credible agent is not going to try to describe the house as something other than what it is. However, the credible agent may talk about the opportunities to renovate the home and significantly increase its value. Similarly, the credible agent is not going to describe their buyer client as eminently qualified if they barely qualify for a loan in the price range where they are looking.

Being a straight shooter is what builds trust between agents. Being friendly and helpful builds a surplus of goodwill that makes the other agent like you and want to help you get the deal done. It also carries over to future transactions with which the two of you may be involved.

What do you do if you are not naturally friendly or you are shy or reserved? The answer is that you try on friendliness like an initially ill-fitting set of clothes and work at it until a new professional demeanor begins to emerge. An easy place to start is to be intentional about how you communicate.

Throughout a transaction, remember to treat the other agent and the parties the way you would want to be treated. Remember to meet them where they are and communicate with them in the way they want. If they call you, call them back. If they text you, text them back. If they email you, email them back. If an agent calls you, and you only text back, that communicates that you don't value them. Also make sure that you respond to all communications promptly, even when they become annoying.

There will be times when you will feel that your efforts to be friendly are neither noticed nor appreciated by the other agent or are met with the opposite of friendliness. In such situations, play a mental game where the goal is to wear the other agent down with your friendliness until she likes you. Again, the primary objective of being friendly should be to build rapport and trust with the other agent. Ideally, you want the other agent to enjoy your conversations and eventually consider you a friend.

How does an agent befriend another agent who may be a stranger or with whom they may have had limited contact? Every agent does it differently, and if you do not know how to be friendly, a career change may be in order. But the common denominator is likely authenticity. So, for example, let's say you try to build rapport by following a predictable pattern of flattering the other agent and asking them lots of questions to get them talking. You may end up befriending them but you also run a risk of appearing fake and formulaic.

Our suggestion is not to be afraid to laugh at yourself and to share things about yourself that make you unique. Of course, all of this is in the context of learning about a property and communicating the positions, issues, and concerns of your respective clients. If you need an icebreaker, there are certain subjects that appear to be of universal interest to agents, "What do you see going on in the market?" or "How is the market treating you at the moment?" usually being at the top of the list.

Unfortunately, some agents, particularly inexperienced ones, mistakenly believe that representing a client requires you to be unfriendly, tough, and aggressive in your interactions with the agent on the other side of the transaction. Nothing could be further from the truth. Some agents who adopt this tough-guy approach do so to avoid being perceived as a pushover. In fact, being friendly has nothing to do with your ability to stand up for your client in a real estate negotiation. Being friendly is really an expression of confidence in your skills and abilities as an agent that you can be yourself regardless of the difficulties that might otherwise arise in the transaction.

Friendliness is a crucial part of an agent's success. If you are difficult, belligerent, or rude during your transactions, you will begin to build a reputation for being unfriendly, and people won't want to work with you. Also, remember to be nice to everybody in the transaction. That includes the other agent, both parties, the lender, the inspector, the appraiser, the title company or attorney, and even the receptionists who answer the phone. People talk, particularly when they are frustrated or offended. If you are ugly to somebody, that is likely to come back to bite you at an inopportune time. Similarly, if you are kind, then people will hear those things about you as well. Always remember, friendliness can make a deal, and a career, as easily as meanness can scuttle it.

Chapter 8

CREDIBILITY, BLUFFING, LYING, AND OTHER ETHICAL ISSUES IN NEGOTIATING

Is IT OKAY for an agent to lie to her counterpart on the other side of a negotiation if it will better the position of the agent's client? Does the saying, "All is fair in love and war" apply to real estate negotiations? Most agents will tell you that the trait they value most in another agent is credibility. This tends to beat out even friendliness, though the two traits are linked. And, when that credibility breaks down, it often means that the breakdown of the negotiation is soon to follow. The most common credibility killer is when an agent is caught in a lie.

Interestingly, the lie does not even have to be particularly material to the transaction for the agent's credibility to be harmed. As previously mentioned, because real estate negotiations are rarely face-to-face, much of the goodwill that is gained from looking somebody in the eye and watching their body language is absent. As a result, once credibility is questioned, it is as good as lost, and the tenor of the negotiation changes. The agent who was lied to is now skeptical of everything she is told. Contract provisions have to be written more carefully to better protect against other possible lies. The extra work significantly increases the risk of the transaction falling apart. Some people back out of transactions altogether if they believe the other party has lied.

The topic of credibility presents several challenges and questions for agents. How does one demonstrate credibility? How do you remain credible yet preserve client confidences? What is the difference between lying, puffing, and bluffing? Is there a way to restore credibility? Let's take a closer look at each of these topics.

Credibility is more about professionalism and straight talk than friendliness. Picture the slickest, most untrustworthy used car salesperson you can imagine. What trait does he most have? The answer is always an exaggerated sense of friendliness. But everything else about him exudes slickness, untrustworthiness, and a lack of credibility. The point is that friendliness without credibility doesn't get negotiations very far.

Being credible means you tell the truth, you do not hide things, and you communicate accurately, completely, and in a straightforward manner. One of the best ways to do that is to volunteer information that is germane to the property or the transaction. So, for example, if the property has flooded twice, the agent and seller should not wait for the buyer's inspector to raise the issue. Aside from the fact that such disclosures are legally required in many states, nondisclosure of relevant information makes it seem as if the seller is trying to hide something.

Instead, the seller's agent should state the facts affirmatively, which are that the house flooded twice. You can then add that there were some extenuating circumstances they may want to be aware of relating to the flooding and information about the steps taken to correct the issue. Agents are going to want to hear about those circumstances, but you establish credibility by first giving them the unvarnished truth.

If you are representing a seller, another way to

establish initial credibility is to become an expert on the property. You should be able to rattle off facts about the house if you're showing it, and you should be able to answer any question a potential buyer or another agent might ask you. If, for example, an agent asks you what type of countertops are in the kitchen, you should be able to answer that question instantly. If you are unable to answer those types of questions with confidence, the buyer and/or their agent might question your expertise and trustworthiness. If, on the other hand, you confidently answer any question they ask, you will look prepared and professional. If that buyer makes an offer, having established yourself in this manner will make anything you say sound more credible. Likewise, if you are representing the buyer, ask thoughtful questions and learn everything you can about the property and the market so that the seller and seller's agent will see you in that same professional and credible light.

Making the job of the other agent easier is also a key to establishing credibility. If you are on the listing side of the transaction, providing things like lead-based paint exhibits, surveys, disclosure statements, and maintenance records for major systems in the home shows that you are not trying to hide anything and are being straightforward. This also suggests that the seller has taken good care of the home. Similarly, if you are representing the buyer, provide information showing that the buyer is financially qualified to purchase the property. All such materials should be presented in an organized fashion to show that your client is reliable and is taking the process seriously.

If you are committed to being credible and always telling the truth, how do you respond to questions where you have either agreed to keep a confidence or where answering might hurt your client's negotiating position? Questions like "Are the sellers getting a divorce?" "Are the sellers in financial trouble?" "What did the other buyer offer?" or "Have you received any offers since the property's been listed?" could all be potentially damaging if answered truthfully. Fortunately, these types of questions can easily be swatted away with a laugh and a hearty, "You know I can't talk about things like that."

There is, of course, no need or obligation ever to reveal your client's position, unless that is what your client wants you to do. Silence can leave the agent on the other side of a transaction as uncertain of your client's position as misrepresenting it, but it is a whole lot safer.

What about the role of puffing and bluffing, if not outright lying? First, you should never lie. It is wrong, and you can risk losing your real estate license. Clearly, however, there are times when bending the truth will better the client's position, but how far is too far? Is it okay, for example, for a buyer's agent to tell a listing agent that the buyer has been looking at other houses when in fact the buyer has not done so? Is it okay for the listing agent to say that there is a lot of other interest in a property when there is very limited interest? Should it make a difference if the agent has been instructed by the seller to make such a statement?

These questions can be hard to answer and endlessly debated. However, our belief is that not telling the truth is a slippery slope, and the more comfortable you get on that slope, the more legal and ethical risks you create for yourself. In a business where your reputation is paramount to your success, a lie could be a deal-killer, both for the transaction and for your career.

If honesty is the best policy, is puffing OK? There is a difference between puffing and lying. Puffing usually involves giving your opinion, which may at times be somewhat exaggerated. Statements like "This is the prettiest street in the neighborhood" or "You won't find a house and yard as nice as this anywhere in town" are examples of puffing but are permissible because they are expressions of opinion. Even saying that there is a lot of interest in the property, regardless of the reality of the situation, can be turned into permissible puffing by saying, "I don't think this property will be on the market for long without being snatched up."

Buyer's agents can also use puffing instead of issuing ultimatums as a bluff during a negotiation. Telling another agent that your buyer is moving on to another house if their offer is not accepted can easily be turned into the truthful statement, "I can't promise that my client won't move on to another house if their offer is not accepted." All that is being said here is that this is a possible outcome of the offer not being accepted. No untruth has been told, and you haven't backed your client into a corner. When it is so easy to tell the truth, to say nothing at all, or to voice opinions, why do anything else?

Once credibility has been lost, there is very little an agent can do to get it back, which is why we suggest being open and honest from the outset. However, there could be times when your credibility, or even your ethics, are questioned because your client has not been forthcoming with you or has changed their position. What do you do?

Depending on the severity of the situation, you have to consider if you want to continue to represent your client. That is a conversation we suggest you have with your broker. Your reputation in real estate is your livelihood, and you do not want to put that at risk over a commission check. If you choose to continue representing your client, then you will need to have a very frank conversation with them about your expectation for honesty. Finally, you will need to tell the other agent the truth. Never make excuses for bad behavior.

Chapter 9

THE DIFFERENT TYPES
OF NEGOTIATORS
YOU WILL LIKELY MEET

AGENTS ARE LIKELY to encounter many different types of negotiators during their careers. Some of the more common ones and how to counter their tactics are discussed below.

The Teaser Negotiator

One common negotiating strategy is for the seller to list the property at a price below where the property is ultimately likely to trade in hopes of soliciting multiple offers from buyers who think there is a deal to be had. The hope is that the competing buyers will bid against one another and drive the final purchase price substantially above the list price. There is a downside risk in employing this strategy in a buyer's market where there are a limited number of buyers. If the low list price doesn't attract enough buyers to drive up the purchase price, then the property may end up selling for less than its true market value.

For buyers negotiating with a seller who is employing this teaser strategy, the best approach is to make a strong offer with a very short time limit that the offer is open to acceptance. The hope for buyers is that the offer is compelling enough that the seller decides to jump at it before the seller has time to receive competing offers.

The Lowball Negotiator

In a normal market, some buyers will make an unusually low offer just to test the seller's commitment to the list price. If the seller makes a counteroffer with a significant reduction in the sales price, it is a sign that the seller likely has room to negotiate and might reduce the price further.

The best response to a lowball strategy is to make only the most modest of price reductions as a way of sending a message that the seller is patient and does not need to make a significant price reduction. If the buyer persists with lowball offers, a conversation with the other agent to let her know of the futility of this approach is in order.

The Bottom Feeder Negotiator

The bottom feeder lives by making multiple very low offers, aggressively resisting increases, aggressively arguing that the offers are indeed good ones, and hoping that an occasional seller will believe her. If the bottom feeder makes fifty offers and goes under contract on even a few, it can be a profitable approach to negotiation. Of course, for the approach to be successful, sellers need to be ignorant of the true value of their properties. Oftentimes, it is the elderly and the poor who end up selling their houses at a below-market price. The best way to fend off the bottom feeders is for the sellers to know the true value of their properties.

The Never-Ending Negotiator

The never-ending negotiator is a person who will not stop negotiating and who just keeps countering what-ever proposal the other party makes. The goal behind this strategy is to wear out the other party and eventually cause her to accept an offer that is far less favorable than what they might otherwise have accepted. The problem in dealing with the never-ending negotiator is that they often only see entering into a contract as a pause in the negotiations. Their intent is to re-trade the deal at a later time.

For example, the never-ending buyer negotiator might counter the price back and forth with a seller a few times and then finally accept the seller's offer knowing that they will be able to negotiate it lower once they inspect the property and submit an amendment to the seller to address defects or other concerns about the property.

The way to deal with the never-ending negotiators is to make a "take it or leave it" offer that doesn't leave room for future negotiations. However, the party making such an ultimatum must be absolutely prepared to walk away from the transaction because the never-ending negotiator's initial response to a "take it or leave it" offer is to seek to negotiate some more. Making the offer an "as-is" offer can also help prevent the never-ending negotiator from trying to use the inspection period as a time to re-trade the deal.

If you are dealing with a never-ending negotiator, you should review the terms of the contract with extra scrutiny to make sure that there are no loose ends or ambiguous terms. Put another way, if every financial issue, large and small, is not thoroughly spelled out in the contract, the never-ending negotiator will seize the opportunity to argue the issue in their favor. Therefore, when dealing with a never-ending negotiator, every financial detail in the contract needs to be tied down.

For example, perhaps you have successfully negotiated that the seller will pay up to $5,000 to cover your buyer's closing costs. Once the settlement statement is sent to the parties, the never-ending negotiator seller will argue what constitutes a closing cost so that they don't have to pay the full $5,000. They will nitpick every fee in order to wear you down so that they come out ahead. If you define closing costs at the outset, however, you limit the never-ending negotiator's ability to continue negotiations.

The Meet-You-in-the-Middle Negotiator

As the name suggests, the meet-you-in-the-middle negotiator will match the price reductions of the other party in hopes of eventually meeting in the middle. So if the seller reduces the sales price by $30,000, the meet-you-in-the-middle negotiator will increase her offer price by $30,000 and continue this pattern until they have met in the middle. The problem with this approach for the seller is that the middle may not have any bearing on the value of the property. A buyer who intends to use this technique would simply need to make a low initial offer so that the "middle" is more favorable to them than it is to the seller. For the buyer, this can be a great approach as it will yield a favorable sales price for the property.

When dealing with a meet-you-in-the-middle negotiator, one question for sellers to consider is whether it makes more sense to make larger reductions in the beginning or the end of the negotiation. The answer usually depends on how the seller has priced the property (and the amount of room the seller has to make price concessions). Generally, sellers should be trying to make smaller concessions in early rounds of offers and counteroffers. Making large price reductions tends to indicate a person who has not thought through the pricing of the property. One of the best options for a seller dealing with this type of negotiator is simply to stop negotiating. A buyer cannot drive the purchase price to an unfavorable middle price if the seller knows their bottom line and refuses to go below it.

The same cannot always be said about the buyer. Buyers will often test the water with a low offer to see how the seller reacts. If the seller, in response to a lowball offer, makes only a small reduction in the price, the buyer will logically need to significantly increase the buyer's offer to get the offer into a range where it might be considered seriously by the seller.

The Precise Negotiator

The precise negotiator starts with an offer that is a round number and successive offers become more specific. So if the first offer is $825,000, the second offer may be $855,000 and the third offer may be $873,250. What is the value of getting more and more specific with offers?

A precise offer conveys a sense that the party using this strategy has carefully thought through exactly what they can offer and is putting their best deal on the table. Such a strategy often works to prevent the party receiving the precise offer from making a counteroffer in a completely different price range. When receiving a precise offer that is not in the right price range, the solution is to make a counteroffer that completely ignores the precise offer and simultaneously ask for an explanation of how the other party's offer was derived. If there is no logical explanation for the offer, it is often a clue that it was just a negotiating ploy.

The Bully Negotiator

The bully tends to negotiate in an overly aggressive and

bullying manner. They come off as a know-it-all and will quickly argue with the agent on the other side as to why their client's offer is a great one and should be immediately accepted. The bully negotiator is dismissive and quick to belittle the rationale of the other party.

The bully often succeeds with less experienced agents who lack confidence and are uncertain as to a property's true value. The bully tends to emphasize their many years of experience pertaining to the positions they take. They may say things like "I've been doing this for thirty years, and I know what a property is going to trade for. This is a great offer but it is not going to last long if it is not accepted right away."

The best strategy for dealing with bullies is to be confident and respond with the facts regarding the value of the property and neighborhood sales history. Never cower in the face of a bully. Do your homework, and believe in your efforts. While there can certainly be disagreements over values, some good comeback lines in response to bullying include "People may value this property differently, but if your buyer wants the property now, they are going to pay the seller's price" or "I hear what you're saying, but this is all my client is prepared to do."

The "My Spouse Is the Difficult One" Negotiator

This is really just a variation of the old good-cop, bad-cop routine. Some people like to make themselves out as far more reasonable than they really are. So, rather than saying that they have a problem with, let's say, whatever concession you recently quoted, they say that they are okay with it, but their wife, partner, or husband is not. To some degree, the good cop is putting himself in a potential mediator's role by then looking for a reasonable compromise between the agent's position and the bad cop's "alleged" position.

Good cop, bad cop routines can be effective because when the good cop agrees with your position, you often feel good about the reasonableness of your approach. It also often makes you more willing to compromise to end the negotiation quickly. Good cop, bad cop routines can be difficult to overcome. Oftentimes, the best approach is to insist that everyone get in the room together to talk through whatever the concerns are. If one partner has been falsely making the other partner the bad guy, meeting together as a group often allows the agent to ferret out what is really happening. This may result in a resolution when the "bad cop" partner will either not play along with the act or it becomes clear that her bad cop position has been overstated.

The other approach is obviously just to stick to your guns and see if the bad guy will not surrender his position.

The "I May Have to Go Elsewhere" Negotiator

This is one of the most common and effective negotiation tactics, particularly in commission negotiations. This negotiator uses the threat of going elsewhere as the leverage for you to reduce your commission. So, this negotiator may say something like "We like your presentation, but the other agent I am considering hiring has offered to list our property for 1 percent less. We are willing to hire you right now, but only if you match the commission being offered by the other agent."

If your potential clients have really talked with another agent, this can be a difficult argument to overcome. But, in some cases, this is just being said without the potential clients having talked with anyone else just to see how you will react.

The first question the agent has to answer when presented with this type of argument is: What are you really willing to work for? If the home is very expensive, a reduction in your commission may be appropriate. If the agent needs the business, a commission reduction may also be appropriate. But if the potential listing does not fall into one of these two categories, reducing your commission may hasten the day when the lower commission amount becomes the new standard.

If you can afford to stand your ground, the best responses are: (1) cheaper real estate agents may not necessarily be as good as you in selling your home and are unlikely to market it as strongly as you will, (2) you believe that with your expertise, network of friends in the business, and the support of your brokerage firm, you can sell their home quicker and at a higher price and that this could more than offset the small difference in commissions being charged by another real estate agent, and (3) if the other agent was willing to reduce their commission so quickly, that is a good indicator that they will be willing to reduce the sales price quickly during a negotiation with a buyer.

The challenge, of course, is that someone good at playing the "I many need to look elsewhere" game may let you walk out the door before either calling you back later to hire you or hiring a lower-priced agent. This is why it is so important to know the prices at which you are willing to work and to walk away if that price is not met.

The Bottom-Line Negotiator

Bottom-line negotiators want to get to the bottom line quickly and have little patience for the back-and-forth of negotiations. They want to name a price and stick to it. Every negotiating strategy works in certain instances, and a bottom-line strategy tends to work best when the bottom-liner has the power in the negotiation. So, in an extreme buyer's market, the bottom-liner may make one offer to buy a property, say it is her best and final, and simply wait for a response. Similarly, in an extreme seller's market, the bottom-liner can announce that her price is the least she will accept, and she is not going to go beneath it.

Bottom-liners tend not to do as well in markets where the relative negotiating power of the parties is more balanced because most buyers and sellers expect the negotiation to go back and forth a bit. In such markets, being a bottom-liner may be more wishful thinking than realistic. The best way to negotiate with a bottom-liner is to treat their alleged bottom line as their opening offer. If you can get the bottom-liner to move off of her bottom line, it indicates that they want to buy or sell (depending on which side of the transaction they are on) the property for more than they are letting on. Once this break in the dam occurs, the bottom-liner will sometimes agree to much deeper price reductions on the selling side and much higher offers on the buying side than what we might normally see in a real estate transaction. This is because the other party can argue that she is just trying to get to the bottom line as quickly as possible as an accommodation to the bottom-liner. Bottom-liners tend to do well when negotiating with other bottom-liners, but only if they are in general agreement on the value of the property.

The Wolf in Sheep's Clothing Negotiator

The wolf in sheep's clothing negotiator holds himself out as unsophisticated when, in fact, he is far more cunning than he lets on. The reality is that some people with whom you are negotiating are dumb, while others are dumb like a fox. Figuring out the difference between the two is not always as easy as it may seem. And, of course, acting unsophisticated is just one of a hundred different ways wolves hide in sheep's clothing.

Why is this type of negotiator effective? The answer is that we sometimes let our guard down with people we perceive to be unsophisticated. When they ask basic and, at times, dumb-sounding questions, we sometimes reveal too much, assuming they will only understand half of what we are saying anyway. Since knowledge is power in a real estate negotiation, this can give the wolf in sheep's clothing negotiator some distinct advantages in the negotiation.

The wolf in sheep's clothing negotiator is also quick to ask for the other agent's help in fashioning solutions to obstacles in the negotiation. Oftentimes, this is done in a way where the other agent ends up negotiating against herself as the wolf in sheep's clothing negotiator explains in an "aw shucks" manner why particular solutions will not work.

So, how do you counter this type of negotiator? The answer is never to underestimate any person with whom you are negotiating and always treat them as more sophisticated than they may seem. When doing this, the wolf in sheep's clothing negotiator often reveals herself to be more sophisticated than she first let on. Agents should also do research on everyone with whom they are negotiating and, if possible, their clients. If an agent is brand-new to the business, the lack of knowledge or sophistication might simply be a sign of their inexperience. If they have been an agent for ten years or so, the naive negotiator routine is more likely an act.

Chapter 10

PUT YOURSELF
IN THE ROLE
OF A MEDIATOR

REAL ESTATE NEGOTIATIONS are somewhat unique in that the agents are negotiating for their clients rather than for themselves. This completely changes the nature of the negotiation and allows the agent to gain an advantage by trying to play the role of a go-between or a mediator.

Maintaining a good relationship with the agent on the other side of the negotiation tends to increase the likelihood of a successful outcome. In negotiating for someone else, the agent can usually maintain a somewhat better relationship with their negotiating counterpart by speaking through the voice of the client who is not partic-ipating directly in the negotiation.

Here's how you do it. First, whenever there is a tough issue that needs to be resolved, the agent should try to discuss it from the client's perspective. A phrase like "I understand your position, but here is the challenge the seller is having" accomplishes this. Of course, if you are going to attribute a position to your client, you'd better confirm with your client that it is indeed their position. Notice that in the mediator's role, the phrase "here is the challenge *my client* is having" is not used. Referring to "my client" creates a separation between you and the other party. Referring to your client as "the buyer" or "the seller" keeps you more in that neutral role.

A good agent negotiator should never say things like

- "I think . . ."
- "I believe . . ."
- "If you ask me . . ."
- "In my opinion . . ."

Instead, the agent should say

- "The seller thinks . . ."
- "The buyer believes . . ."
- "The seller appears to be concerned about . . ."

Let's look at the following example to better understand this concept of speaking through the voice of your
client. Consider how you would react as a listing agent
if the buyer's agent in trying to negotiate a significant
price reduction were to say something like "I've looked
at the comps and the price the seller wants, and it's just
not realistic or justified." Now, while that statement is
certainly reasonable, you now become the obstacle to
getting the deal done. Consciously or subconsciously,
you became the stumbling block. There may even be a
twinge of resentment toward you for doing your job so
well. Because it is a statement of your position, you also
open the door to an argument about the correctness of
your position.

Now, let's replay the scenario, but with the agent
speaking through the voice of the buyer. The buyer's agent
in trying to negotiate a significant price reduction now
says something like "Before making an offer, the buyer
had me pull all of the comparables in the neighborhood.
It created a concern for the buyer. After studying them,
the buyer indicated that they just cannot justify making
an offer higher than the one she has made. I understand
the seller wants more for their property. All sellers do. The

buyer has, unfortunately, indicated that she is not going to budge on the price."

There is a subtle difference between the two approaches. In the second scenario, the agent appears to be not so much negotiating as reporting. And what is being reported is not particularly good news. But look how easy it is to report bad news when you are not the one justifying your view that the seller's price is too high but are merely reporting the buyer's position.

Speaking through the buyer or seller makes it much easier to communicate difficult messages. It can also avoid arguments. If the listing agent now wants to get into a fight over the comparables, you can easily sidestep a dispute by simply saying she has made some good points, and you will present them to your client. This then keeps you in that go-between position and sets up a future round of negotiations where, if need be, you can say, "I presented the information to the buyer, and here is the challenge the buyer is having." There may even be times where you will later make a concession based on the good information the other agent has presented. All of this can be done without a fight.

The point is that being a good advocate for your

client's position does not necessarily mean that you have to be argumentative. You can explain your client's position in the detached manner of a go-between, make the same points, and limit your role with the other agent to that of a messenger. And, of course, it then gives you a "Don't shoot the messenger" defense if the other agent does not respond well to whatever you are telling them.

In the mediator's role, the agent does not have to judge any of the offers or counteroffers being made by the other party. She can be neutral about all of them and indicate that the decision is for the seller (or buyer, as the case may be) to make. If the offer or counteroffer is rejected, she can explain why and communicate what the other party has said it will take to get the deal done.

Are you throwing your client under the bus by attributing the tough positions to them? Not really. The statements being attributed to your client are in fact the positions of your client. Moreover, merely saying "here is the challenge my client is having" is not exactly throwing the client under the bus. Finally, if the other agent now views your client as possibly difficult, it is nothing that any experienced agent hasn't seen a thousand times before or, frankly, come to expect.

Acting as a mediator also opens the door for the agents to work together to find a solution to take back to their respective clients. By collaborating with the other agent to find solutions, you often learn more about the issues that matter most to the other party. Understanding motivations can help you figure out a way that both buyer and seller can achieve their respective goals. Sometimes, this means sharing your own client's motivations with the other agent—with permission, of course. You might say something like "My client has said that one of her biggest concerns is getting settled into her new house before school starts. If your buyer is willing to move the closing date up by a week, I might be able to get the seller to agree to purchase the home warranty that your buyer wants."

Remember, however, that as a mediator, you must make it clear to the other agent that you cannot make decisions for your client. Therefore, it's good to use noncommittal phrases like "I will present your position to my client, but, of course, I can't promise how they will respond . . ." This shows that you are actively working toward finding a resolution, but your client is the one who has the final say.

Chapter 11

KEEP FOCUSED
ON THE BIG PICTURE

BUYERS AND SELLERS often get their backs up over items the value of which are miniscule compared to the purchase price of a house. One party or the other essentially gets stubborn over $500 and refuses to make a repair, increase the amount of a counteroffer, or agree to leave something in the house. No matter how much you try to cajole your client, the buyer or seller tells you that they have been pushed too far, and they just have to put their foot down. Economically, this absolutely makes no sense. So why do parties do this?

The short answer is likely pride, stubbornness, and ego in having to go further than they wanted to go. Moreover, $500 is, well, $500. It is not a lot of money

when factored into the price of a home, but it is a lot of walking-around money. Consumers start to think about the things they could buy with $500 and get stubborn when they feel like they have been pressed to the limit.

Good negotiators therefore try to keep their clients focused on $500 being an inconsequential amount in buying a house and away from thinking about it as spending money. One way to do this is to always keep a mortgage calculator with you so that you can show your client what $500 is once amortized over fifteen or thirty years. And, just to complete the exercise, let's look at the chart below to see what the monthly payment is on $500 at interest rates of 3, 6, and 9 percent over fifteen and thirty years.

	3%	6%	9%	
Amoritization of $500 at different interest rates	$3.00	$4.00	$5.00	15 years
	$2.00	$3.00	$4.00	30 years

It is basically the cost of a cup of coffee or two every month.

When parties are forced to focus on the amortization of $500, most quickly concede that, in the grand scheme of things, they are being unreasonable. The response of the party is then often, "Well, it's the principle of the thing" often coupled with, "When is it going to end if I don't put my foot down now?"

To close the deal here, you are negotiating not only with the other party but with your own client as well. The concern of your client as to "when is it going to end" is a legitimate one. After all, $500 here and $500 there and pretty soon it can start to add up to real money.

One strategy for dealing with this is to signal the other agent that your client is at their limit in the negotiation. You can then let the other agent know that you might be able to convince your client to make one small final concession if the other agent can get with her client and confirm that the parties will have a deal if it is accepted. If the other agent can give you that assurance, you can tell your client the assurances you have received and, hopefully, convince your client that this will really bring the negotiation to a close. If the other agent cannot give that assurance, then this may be a transaction that just was not meant to be.

In trying to keep your client focused on the big picture, it is always smart to remind your client that (1) every counteroffer terminates all previous offers and counteroffers and (2) having done so, the other party is free to walk away from the transaction such that your client will never hear from them again.

It is always a total shock to most clients, usually sellers, when the other party walks away from the transaction entirely over some small counteroffer. Usually, their first reaction when they realize what happened is to try to retract their last counteroffer. But, alas, in most, if not all, states this is not possible to do. The question that should be asked of buyers and sellers is whether a counteroffer for a small amount is worth the risk of losing the deal entirely. Fortunately, in most instances when a counteroffer is made for a small amount, the transaction remains intact. However, it is a mighty letdown when one party or the other pushes just a little too far. This is another good reason for agents to signal the other when their client has reached or is about to reach their breaking point.

Chapter 12

LEARN THE VALUE
OF PATIENCE

FOR THE PERSON with leverage in a negotiation, doing
nothing or moving slowly is often a great negotiation
tactic. What does this mean? Let's say it is an extreme
seller's market. The buyers really want the house and
make a good offer. However, they have not put all of their
money on the table, wanting to hold something back, if
possible. How does the seller use patience to get them to
make a higher offer?

The answer for the listing agent is to give a noncommittal response that doesn't drive the buyer away but
nevertheless leaves them feeling insecure. So, the listing
broker might say something like "The seller appreciated
your client's offer. There has been a lot of interest in the

property and the seller is thinking about how best to proceed."

How does this approach benefit the seller? When most buyers make an offer, they want to know instantly whether it is going to be accepted or not. We live in a fast-paced world where instant gratification has generally become the norm. When people have to wait for things, especially things they really want, they become impatient. Buying a home is one of the most important decisions most people will make in their lives. When they get to the point of making an offer on a particular home, they almost immediately begin envisioning what it would be like to live in that house and in that neighborhood. Having to wait to know whether they will get that chance can make some buyers a little crazy, and for some, a lot crazy.

This impatience can lead to two results. If the buyer feels like it is a hopeless cause, they may go elsewhere. But if the buyer wants the house badly enough, the buyer can end the wait (or at least try to) by putting a better offer on the table. Perhaps that was the seller's goal all along.

Of course, this works only when a party has leverage in the transaction. In an extreme seller's market, if the buyer were to tell the seller he was going to think about whether to make an offer or not, the seller would laugh and go on to the next buyer in the line of buyers waiting to purchase the property. The best way for an agent to address the impatience issue is to encourage your clients to be patient, explain that it is normal for the other side to need time to evaluate any offer, and try to have them set realistic expectations.

Sellers can also become impatient when their property sits on the market for a couple of weeks, and they start to wonder why it hasn't sold yet. In an extreme seller's market, this frustration can arise after just a few days. Had the agent taken the time to educate the client on what they should reasonably expect (and then given them a lot of reassurance along the way that this time delay is normal and not something to worry about), the client's impatience may have been kept to a minimum. If a buyer or seller has an expectation that something will take a particular amount of time, they do not worry as much, at least until the time period you have set has elapsed.

More than anything, one party's patience can help reset the expectations of the other party, but it does so at the risk of losing the deal altogether. To better understand this, let's say that the seller turns down a buyer's offer of $700,000, and the buyer makes no further offers. A month now goes by and no other buyers have made any offer to buy the property. To the seller, the $700,000 offer is starting to look better and better. The passage of time and the buyer's patience helped to reset the seller's expectations. Of course, a week after the buyer went silent, another buyer could have come along, offered $725,000, and bought the house out from under the first buyer. Patience can reset expectations, but it does so only if the buyer can live with the risk of not getting the property at all.

This underscores one of the fundamental principles of negotiation. The more risk a party is willing to live with, the greater the likelihood the party will win big. But in accepting more risk, the party must also be willing to lose big. Most buyers and sellers do not have the temperament for such high-risk strategies. If a buyer likes a house and has to pay more than she had hoped to acquire it, most buyers will bite the bullet and pay more. The same is true with sellers in reverse. Most are willing to accept a little less than they had hoped. But to the risk-takers usually go the greatest rewards and the biggest losses.

Most great negotiators know that slowing down the negotiation, whenever that is possible, keeps parties guessing, makes them nervous, and makes them more willing to commit. Now, of course, the above suggestion does not apply in extreme markets. And if it is not possible to slow them down a lot, it is always good to slow them down a little.

An agent friend recently told us about a seller who received a good offer but not a great offer. He wanted to counter within fifteen minutes of receiving it.

"I almost had to tie him in a chair to prevent him from sending the counter," she said. "No matter how hard I tried, I just could not convince him that he might seem a tad anxious if he countered within fifteen minutes."

"Well, I am anxious," he replied.

"Yes, I get that," she said, "but the point is that you want the buyer to think that you are just not sure what to do about his counteroffer and are struggling to decide. Appearing anxious sends a message that you are anxious to wrap things up and might take less."

Finally, he got it and waited until the next day to send his counteroffer.

Chapter 13

LEARN THE VALUE OF PERSISTENCE

THOMAS EDISON once said that "many of life's failures are people who did not realize how close they were to success when they gave up." Persistence, particularly in a market where the buyer and seller have about the same negotiating power, is something that can pay off big in negotiations. Here's why.

Most real estate is worth different things to different people. Its ultimate sales price can be somewhere within a range of values. As a result, most sellers are never quite sure of the price at which their property will trade. Human nature being what it is, they tend to estimate its value at the higher end of that range because that maximizes their return. If the seller gets a low offer, his or her initial reaction is often anger and an immediate rejection of the offer. But if no other offers are made for the property, doubt often starts to creep in about the property's true value. "Maybe my property is not really worth what I thought" is the operative thought here. A seller's situation might also change as time passes. Perhaps the sellers have found a new home they want to purchase, so whereas they were able to be patient before, now they are motivated to sell.

Of course, the process of the seller developing a more realistic sense of the value of the property can take weeks, if not months. It is difficult for a buyer to anticipate the seller's changing situation. If the buyer's offer has been rejected, being persistent in communicating an interest in the property (but at the buyer's lower price point) can sometimes win the day if the buyer's communication of his or her continued interest coincides with the seller rethinking what she is willing to take for the property.

The trick is to figure out how to (1) show this persistence without alienating the listing agent or the seller and (2) create a sense of urgency on the part of the seller to reduce his or her price to a more realistic number.

Normally, it makes sense to let some time go by after the buyer's offer has been rejected to let the seller start to rethink the value of the property and confirm that no higher offers will be forthcoming from the buyer. If, after the seller has not received any other offers, the buyer resurfaces, the seller may be thrilled that the buyer is still in the picture. If the buyer increases his or her offer just a bit, it may reopen the door to negotiations in the buyer's lower price range. Continuing this dance over a period of additional weeks can allow the seller's position to evolve on the value of his or her property. The buyer's agent should regularly communicate that the buyer remains interested in the property, but only at the lower price.

To avoid annoying the listing agent, texting or emailing may be the way to go to express a simple message like "Hey, if the seller comes down some more on the price for the property, I think we can get a deal done." This strategy requires an abundance of patience and a willingness to lose the property if another buyer at a higher price comes along. Buyer's agents should listen carefully to any clues the seller's agent might give about the seller's changing circumstances. Being a good listener is a key part of persistence.

Of course, if the seller is still not being realistic or, depending on your perspective, if the buyer continues to make unrealistically low offers, the buyer's agent should clearly communicate to the listing agent that the buyer is finally going to move on and try to find a different house. It would still make sense for the buyer's agent to ask the seller's agent to please stay in touch. This may help create the sense of urgency without sounding like a threat. This sense of urgency might just be what is needed for the seller to make the kind of significant price reduction to get the transaction closed.

Persistence on the part of the buyer is a negotiating strategy that mostly works in a buyer's market or a shifting market, but even then, the probability of success is low. Many sellers simply have a price that they will not go below. But persistence in real estate negotiations reflects a wonderful and successful philosophy on the part of agents never to give up in a negotiation and to keep looking for common ground. Sometimes, ways to close gaps in a real estate transaction are not always initially obvious. It often takes repeated conversations, a lot of listening, and running ideas up the flagpole with the other agent and your client for the parties to finally come to a solution that will allow the transaction to move forward. In the transactions where things fall into place and a transaction gets done, it is well worth it.

Chapter 14

CREATING POSITIVE LEVERAGE

DURING A NEGOTIATION, having leverage means having power. The party with the most leverage typically comes out on the more favorable end of a negotiation. As we mentioned in the introduction, the market often dictates the initial leverage in a real estate transaction. Understandably, a seller will have more negotiating power in an extreme seller's market, and a buyer will have more negotiating power in an extreme buyer's market. This happens because the party favored by the extreme market has sufficient favorable alternatives such that they do not have to become invested in making one particular deal work over another.

In more balanced markets and in later stages of a

negotiation, leverage—and thus, negotiating power—often gets volleyed back and forth between buyer and seller. The words that the agents use to communicate can increase or decrease the amount of leverage their client has. The person with the leverage can change on a dime with the twists, turns, and surprises that often accompany real estate transactions.

If a party has appealing alternatives, such as other good properties that the buyer can buy or other buyers to whom the seller can sell, then their mindset and approach to the negotiation will be different than the party who has fewer or less appealing options. The operative word in that sentence being *mindset* because what someone believes can sometimes be as important, if not more important, than actual market conditions. A seller who is in no hurry to move, for example, gives up less leverage in an extreme buyer's market than a seller who is trying to move quickly. Always keep in mind that a person's emotions and situation help shape their mindset at any given point in time.

Agents must master the ability to use scripts and strategies to shift mindsets in a way that keeps the leverage power ball in their client's court no matter what type of market they encounter. They must learn to identify and communicate favorable alternatives for their client and to highlight poor alternatives for the party on the opposite side of the transaction. In essence, they must gently direct both parties to adopt mindsets that will ultimately benefit their client the most.

Consider the leveraging strength in the messaging behind the following statements:

1. *"My buyers absolutely love this house and want to buy it."*

This statement may help get the buyers the house, but it also sends a message that the seller can extract a higher price. Generally speaking, an agent using this sort of statement is handing the seller leverage on a silver platter. If, however, the agent believes that the sellers are looking for a buyer who will love the house as much as they do, then this statement might actually make the buyer's offer more appealing than competing offers. Offering the other party something they want is a way of creating positive leverage. An agent who has asked the right questions and made careful observations will know if this is a smart tactic to employ.

2. *"My buyers absolutely love this house. At the right price, it could be their first choice."*

This statement is a little stronger. It still communicates great interest in the house but introduces a good price as a condition of reaching the favorable outcome. The seller will likely need to concede something to get the deal done. In the right market, dangling this sort of carrot in front of a seller might be a clever strategy.

3. *"My buyers really like this house. Of course, inventory is increasing, and there are several houses that look like they might work. They are very sensitive to price."*

This statement expressly uses market conditions to shift the leverage to the buyer. The agent is sending a clear message that the price will need to be good for the buyer to buy. That being said, if the seller has other options to sell the property, the seller may choose a different buyer. The buyer's agent and the buyer need to be sensitive to the realities of the market in deciding the tone of the statements they make, particularly in their early negotiations. If the buyer's agent in an extreme seller's market were to talk about increased inventory and the buyer being price sensitive, the listing agent would likely laugh.

In addition to considering the market, you also have to consider how risk-adverse your client is. There is often a relationship between the degree of risk a party is willing to take and the amount of leverage they stand to gain. Statement 3 above risks losing the deal for the buyer. But, in the right circumstances, the buyer will have greater leverage as a result of using this statement than she might have otherwise had. For the right buyer, this is a risk worth taking.

How the listing agent responds to these statements sends a message back to the buyer's agent in the elaborate dance of trying to get a deal done. Consider these responses to news that the buyer will be making an offer:

1. *"I am thrilled to hear the buyer is going to be making an offer. I know the sellers are ready to sell, and I will present your offer as soon as I receive it."*

This statement sends a message that the seller is motivated (maybe even desperate) to sell. There is no play to shift the leverage to the seller, so the buyer retains their power position.

2. *"I will wait for your offer. My clients aren't in a hurry to sell, so it's hard to predict how they will react, but I hope we will be able to reach an agreement."*

This is a relatively neutral statement and doesn't reveal much about what the seller's reaction might be. It does, however, hint that the sellers will reject, or at least counter, the buyer's offer if it is for less than the list price. In doing so, the listing agent is telling the buyer that she is in a vulnerable position, which helps create a sense of urgency for the buyer who will be left wondering what the seller's reaction might be. As we will discuss later in this book, creating urgency is a great way to obtain leverage.

3. *"There is a lot of interest in this house, and we are expecting multiple offers. If your buyer wants this house, I hope she puts her best offer on the table right away."*

This message introduces competition in order to shift the leverage back to the seller and lets the buyer know that she will not be able to get many seller concessions. If the listing agent is running a bluff, and there aren't other interested parties, this approach may backfire. Some buyers will back out simply because they don't want to get into a bidding war. But if the agent is bluffing and the gamble works, the buyer might make a better offer because they feel like they have less room to negotiate.

The beauty of real estate is that both buyer and

seller have something positive to gain from making the transaction happen. The seller has a property that the buyer wants, and the buyer has the money that the seller wants. Gentle reminders about the benefits available from making a deal happen can help the parties move beyond sticking points in the negotiation. When focused on the benefits of a transaction instead of the obstacles, it is easier to find solutions to most problems.

For example, let's say a negotiation has stalled over a disagreement about the amount of closing costs the sellers will pay on behalf of the buyer. If the buyer's agent knows that the sellers are trying to move because their current home is too far from their child's school, then the buyer's agent could say something like "You mentioned that the sellers are moving to be closer to their daughter's school. My client is ready to buy now. If the sellers can work with us on this issue, they can close before the start of the school year." Reminding a party about the benefits to be gained by making a deal work can be a powerful motivator.

Chapter 15

THE VALUE OF NEGATIVE LEVERAGE

LEVERAGE CAN ALSO be used negatively in a negotiation. This happens when one party presents an unfavorable alternative or consequence that the opposing party will face if that opposing party does not accept the proposed terms. For example, a seller might say to a buyer that they will not sell the house to the buyer unless the buyer pays the full list price. This sort of ultimatum introduces a negative alternative into the mix. An agent might also create negative leverage by pointing out that the other party's alternatives are more limited or less favorable than they might imagine. As we will discuss later, ultimatums should be used judiciously and with forethought.

Time, like money, is a valuable commodity in a

negotiation, and introducing the risk of losing time and/or money is one of the easiest ways to use negative leverage to your advantage. No matter how many alternatives exist, the longer a home has been under contract, the more invested in the deal the parties are likely to become. Starting over can be painful for buyers and sellers alike. Additionally, if a buyer has already paid for an appraisal, survey, and/or inspection, or if a seller has already made buyer-specific repairs, then alternatives become more costly. In poker, this is called being "pot committed." A player has so much invested in the hand, that it makes more sense to keep moving forward than it does to fold. Remembering this, smart agents can use contract time and financial investment to their advantage during later stages of a negotiation.

During the early stages of a negotiation, however, the ability to use negative alternatives as leverage takes a bit more skill. Let's say buyer Paula and seller Paul sign a contract that contains a ten-day inspection period that gives Paula the right to terminate without penalty during that time period at her sole discretion. On the ninth day, Paula's inspection report reveals multiple defects in the property that need to be fixed. Paula's agent sends the seller's agent an amendment for the seller to agree to make repairs.

The buyer's agent says, "The buyer still wants the house, but she would like the seller to fix the defects on the amendment I just sent." This statement successfully communicates the message, but it does nothing to maximize the buyer's bargaining power. That might be a good thing depending on the nature of the transaction. If the buyer's agent has taken the time to speak with the agent on the other side, she might know the circumstances behind a seller's decision to sell and be able to anticipate the seller's reaction to the buyer's request to fix the defects.

If the agent wants to try to shift leverage to the buyer in this example, she would likely need to take a different approach. Perhaps she might say, "My buyer is very concerned about the number of defects and is not sure whether to proceed with the contract. I hope the seller will quickly commit to correcting the defects so that we can keep this transaction together."

This sends a much stronger message and will likely be received differently than the first option. The message to the seller is that agreeing to correct the defects is essential and not doing so may kill the deal. Sending too strong a message that the buyer may terminate could make the seller angry and deter them from making any repairs, particularly if the defects are minor. Similarly, if the seller has a backup offer waiting, it is early enough in the transaction that they might opt to let the deal terminate. That is a risk that the agent and buyer will carefully need to weigh against the benefit of gaining leverage.

If the seller in this scenario has a backup offer, the seller might be able to use that to shift the buyer's mindset. Letting the buyer know that there are one or multiple buyers waiting to buy the property would neutralize the buyer's ability to use the threat of a lawful termination to negotiate a better position.

Instead of using an ultimatum in this case, the buyer's agent could have taken a softer approach to preempt any arguments the seller might make about backup offers. For example, she might say, "The buyer's requests are very reasonable, and I think you will agree that any buyer interested in buying the property would ask the seller to make these repairs. Your seller might have had other interest in the property, but if they have to start over, they will lose time and likely end up right back in this same spot." Gently pointing out that the seller's alternatives are not as favorable as they might think is an approach that is less likely to anger the seller and will hopefully reinforce the seller's investment in the deal already on the table.

There are three main concepts to remember about leverage. First, there are nuances in every negotiation, and finding the right balance between leveraging a party and alienating that party can be a fine one. An agent should always discuss the risks and benefits of each course of action with their client.

Second, the words and tone an agent uses matter. They should hopefully match the goals and desires of the agent's client so that the agent's aggressiveness and efforts to create leverage do not inadvertently cost their client the deal. This is why understanding the position of a client and their tolerance for risk is so important.

Lastly, understanding the market and asking lots of questions can help the agent know, or at least predict, what will motivate the other party. Understanding that motivations shift and change as the parties' investments in the transaction increase is equally important. That knowledge can help their client determine if a more aggressive position is a risk worth taking.

Chapter 16

CREATING A SENSE OF URGENCY

THE DECISION to buy or sell a house is a big one, and when confronted with big decisions, some people have a hard time making decisions quickly. Getting buyers and sellers to act is something that agents work hard to do. Timing is often used as a means of creating leverage in a contract negotiation, so getting the other side to speed up their normal decision-making process is another important skill for agents to master.

One way this is done is to give the other party a short period of time to respond to offers and counteroffers. Over the last several decades, the amount of time given for people to decide whether to accept or reject an offer or counteroffer has shrunk tremendously (and many would say unreasonably). If an offer or counteroffer is made in the morning, there is a growing expectation for the other side to respond by day's end.

For buyers, the risk is that the seller will receive a competing offer that is better than theirs or that the seller will share the terms of the buyer's offer with competitors in an effort to drive up the sales price. By reducing the amount of time a seller has to respond to the offer, a buyer can minimize these risks. A seller who believes the old adage about "a bird in the hand" might be motivated to act instead of waiting to see if they will receive additional offers. The shortened time frame for acceptance of the buyer's offer creates a sense of urgency, and therefore gives the buyer leverage.

So how does a seller combat this? In an extreme seller's market, it isn't uncommon for a seller's agent to notify all buyers in advance that they will not consider or respond to any offers until a specific day and time. They instruct buyer's agents not to include shortened acceptance periods if they want their offer to be considered. By preempting the buyer's ability to use abbreviated time limits in their offers, their seller can maintain leverage. The other added benefit of this sort of strategy is that some buyers are motivated to make stronger offers because they are anticipating competition. The seller may never receive any other offers, but the pressure would be no less real to the buyer.

Sellers should use caution, however. When told that offers will not be considered until a specific day and time, some buyer's agents will hold off making their offer until the eleventh hour. By doing so, they stop the seller from using their offer to drive competing offers, and they keep the seller wondering about how strong their position really is. As previously discussed, some buyers simply won't make an offer at all because they do not want to get into a bidding war. Sellers should also use caution because they risk losing a strong offer that comes in early. By waiting to accept a strong offer, the buyer is given time to withdraw it.

In a more normalized market, the best way to combat a short time frame in an offer is just to ignore it. If a seller intends on making a counteroffer, the expiration of the original offer isn't of much consequence. Of course, if the seller accepts a buyer's offer after it has expired, that is, in most if not all jurisdictions, a counteroffer that must then be accepted by the buyer.

Like buyers, sellers can also use the abbreviated acceptance period strategy with counteroffers. This may or may not be a beneficial strategy. If the seller believes that more buyers are likely to make offers, then dragging out the counteroffer process might give them leeway to withdraw the offer if a better one comes along before the buyer has accepted it. On the other hand, if a seller has made an aggressive counteroffer, leaving it open for acceptance for only a short period of time might push the buyer into making a quick decision that is more favorable to the seller. The shortened time for acceptance, in combination with the strong counteroffer, communicates that the seller might also have a strong alternative.

People sometimes do not think through things very carefully if they are being forced to make a decision quickly. When someone is being pushed, it is natural for their anxiety to increase. If the buyer really wants the property and is worried about losing out to another buyer, that anxiety could translate into an acceptance of a counteroffer that they might not have accepted otherwise. Competition is a big motivator for many buyers.

Some seller's brokers will try to create urgency through competition by intentionally inviting multiple buyers to see a property at the same time or having over-lapping showings in hopes that it will motivate one of the potential buyers to act quickly. Others will simply mention that there is a lot of interest in the property. Holding an open house is another way to create urgency if an interested buyer believes that lots of other potential buyers will see the house and it may therefore slip away.

While these tactics can motivate some people, they can also backfire. If, for example, it looks like the listing agent intentionally scheduled overlapping showings to pressure the buyer, it can hurt the credibility of the seller's broker in the eyes of the buyer. Other buyers may simply walk away out of annoyance. Of course, in an extreme seller's market, most properties are sold after multiple offers are made on the property, and this is simply the reality of that type of market.

A sense of urgency can be created in any number of other ways, including, interestingly enough, giving the impression that no deal can be done. An agent recently told us of a situation where a seller was having a difficult time selling an expensive but dated house. A buyer finally came along and was willing to buy the house and to update it, but the buyer was willing to do so only if the purchase was contingent on the sale of the buyer's house. The buyer was willing to include a kick-out clause in case another buyer came along. The seller did not want to agree to the contingency, and the agents went back and forth without success while looking for a solution. Finally, the buyer's agent thanked the other agent for her hard work and said it looked like it was just a bridge too far to try to get a deal done and that her buyers were going to move on. It wasn't an ultimatum inviting a concession. It was a statement of finality closing the door to further negotiation.

The agent said this with her buyers' permission, who still wanted the house but were unwilling to buy it until they sold their existing home. When the sellers finally realized that they were about to lose the buyers, they quickly came back and agreed to the contingency. An agent thanking the other agent and saying that they were moving on turned out to have a remarkable effect in creating urgency on the part of the other party.

Creating a sense of urgency is a powerful negotiation strategy, but agents should discuss the pros and cons of such strategies with their clients before taking steps to implement them.

Chapter 17

LEARN TO SIZE UP
THE PARTIES

NOT ALL NEGOTIATIONS will end the way you expect them
to end. Some will turn out better than you expect, others
worse. This happens because real estate negotiations deal
with every type of person imaginable, from irrational
to rational, emotional to unemotional, smart to not so
smart, sophisticated to unsophisticated, and the full range
of every human trait.

The trick is to try to evaluate the personality traits
of the people with whom we are interacting and tailor
our negotiating strategy accordingly. It is usually easier
to evaluate the sellers because we get to see their houses.
The price of a house and its location, condition, furniture, artwork, and decor can sometimes tell us about the

owner's financial well-being, degree of sophistication, and how they might negotiate.

The emphasis here should be on *sometimes*. Obviously, there are very sophisticated people who live in modest homes. Depersonalizing homes and staging have also made it harder to know as much about the seller as we once did. But even in walking through a staged and depersonalized home, we can make some snap judgments about the people we will be negotiating with that can give us preliminary ideas about how to negotiate with them.

The other way we glean valuable information is to ask questions of the listing agent. The question, "Who are the sellers, and why are they selling?" should always be asked. If the sellers have already bought and closed on another house, it may tell us that the sellers may not drive quite as hard a bargain as someone who must sell before they can even consider another house.

A seller who is an elderly widower might not be the person to whom we want to present a very complex offer with lots of difficult-to-understand contingencies. A seller with an accounting or engineering diploma on the wall may be focused not only on the price of the home but on how each of the costs in the transaction affect that price. Similarly, a law school diploma might suggest that the seller will be as focused on the words in the contract as on the financial terms of the transaction.

A home with lots of maintenance needs or in very poor physical condition might tell us that the seller is experiencing financial difficulties. Again, we emphasize "*might* tell us" because these are nothing more than the most preliminary hunches about people that may later prove to be true or false.

Many agents unconsciously make these preliminary judgments without even realizing it. They then modify their judgments as the negotiation progresses, and they have had a chance to see how the other party reacts to different offers and counteroffers. The key is to try to be more consciously aware of the little details and use them to your advantage.

Chapter 18

FILTER COMMUNICATIONS TO KEEP THE DEAL ON TRACK

ONE OF THE FIRST concepts we addressed in this book is that residential real estate negotiations are particularly challenging because buyers and sellers rarely negotiate face-to-face. As such, these negotiations, at least to some degree, take place in a vacuum without the benefit of those critical social cues that foster understanding. Instead, the parties negotiate at a distance through agent intermediaries.

Even the agents generally do not negotiate with one another face-to-face. Like the parties, they might not meet in person until the day of closing, if ever. Sometimes, their interactions prior to closing are limited to text, email, and phone calls. That means that not only are the parties unable to use contextual clues to help them understand the opposing party's words but they often have limited positive personal knowledge of the players to help fill in the gaps.

As a result, two things tend to happen. First, the parties sometimes misinterpret each other's intentions. Second, whatever information they receive from their agent about the other party is often magnified and blown out of proportion. The agent's opinion is given more weight than what it otherwise might have been given because it is one of the few sources of available information.

So, for example, if you tell your buyer that the seller is difficult, the client tends to think they are really difficult. That will likely make negotiations more challenging. The opposing party will form similar impressions based on how messages are delivered. Therefore, filtering what you say, both to your client and to the opposing party, can be beneficial. Let's start with how to speak to your own client.

To prevent the transaction from going off the rails, try to avoid complaining to your client about the opposing party or their agent. This does not mean, of course, that you cannot answer basic questions that might get asked by your client about the other agent. If the other agent is new to the business or very experienced, it is okay to explain that to your client. However, if you have nothing nice to say about the other agent, say nothing at all. You should also filter as much of the opposing party's negativity out of the communications to your client as possible.

For instance, say the buyer's agent tells you, "My clients thinks the seller is totally unrealistic. The house is way overpriced. In its present poor condition, my client is only willing to offer $480,000." You could certainly share this feedback with your client verbatim, but the seller is likely to become defensive, if not offended. That wouldn't do much to foster productive negotiations.

You are more likely to get an open-minded response from your client if you say, "The buyer is only willing to offer $480,000." With this statement, the seller gets the facts but not the commentary that might trigger an emotional or angry response. Filtering is an extremely important way to keep the parties engaged and hopefully prevent anger from festering.

Next, let's examine how you can help negotiations when speaking to the opposing party. In contrast to how buyers and sellers negotiate through agent intermediaries, many other business negotiations are face-to-face where the parties first go through a ritual of getting to know one another before getting down to the actual negotiation. Everyone is usually on their best behavior as they talk about their backgrounds and their businesses, and exchange pleasantries. While such small talk may seem of little value, it actually serves an extremely important social purpose of creating goodwill and rapport between the parties. This helps build the foundation needed to allow the parties to have a degree of trust that is essential to a successful business relationship. As one business executive explained, "Before I get down to business with a person, I want to make sure that person is someone with whom I want to do business."

The point is that building goodwill and rapport through direct contact with a person on the other side of a business negotiation helps set the deal in motion and keeps it together as the parties work through difficult business issues. So, how do you do that in a real estate transaction where the buyer and seller are communicating only through agent intermediaries?

The answer is that it is often difficult, and the absence of rapport and goodwill results in many transactions falling apart. However, a great agent negotiator can help foster some degree of trust between the parties by building up the image of their client whenever possible in conversations with the other agent. Even making little comments such as the following can help build a positive image of your client with the other agent, some of which will hopefully be communicated to the other agent's client.

1. My clients are such nice people.

2. My clients are so easy to work with.

3. My clients are such reasonable people. They are a delight.

4. I am sure we can work through this issue. My clients always try to be fair.

5. My clients have done everything they have said they were going to do.

Sometimes, repetition makes it so. If the agent representing a party regularly communicates how fair and reasonable their client is, it can help form a positive impression of the party in the eyes of the other agent and their client in subsequent conversations. If the negotiation becomes strained down the road, this positive image can be the factor that keeps the deal together.

Now, you may be wondering why buyers and sellers do not actually negotiate face-to-face at some point.

When we asked agents this question, most said that it would be an unmitigated disaster both because issues would get missed and because far fewer deals would get done without agents filtering out negativity and aggression. In other words, though challenging, negotiating at a distance through intermediaries serves a positive purpose.

The wide variation in the sophistication of the parties, the emotional aspects of buying and selling a house, and the diametrically opposed goals of the seller to sell the home for as high a price as possible versus the buyer wanting to pay as little as possible for the house can quickly lead to major disputes. The unspoken truth is that clients sometimes have difficult personalities; keeping them hidden in the background from the other party for as long as possible increases the likelihood of a deal getting done.

That is not to say that a face-to-face meeting cannot be of great benefit in certain circumstances. If the parties reach an impasse, sometimes sitting down together will allow them to understand the other side's perspective more clearly. Also, sometimes the agent on the other side of the transaction could be doing a poor job articulating your client's position. If you suspect that to be the case, a face-to-face meeting might be the solution.

Chapter 19

TRY TO ENLIST THE OTHER AGENT'S HELP

IF BUILDING RAPPORT with the other agent is at the top of most agents' lists for how to be a successful negotiator, learning to enlist their help is one of the payoffs for establishing that rapport. People like helping others when they can easily do so. If you learn how to ask for help in the right way, you are oftentimes rewarded for your efforts.

Several successful agents we interviewed said they always call other agents to tell them that their clients are making an offer and to ask what the sellers would consider a perfect offer. While the initial response of the listing agent is often a joking suggestion of an all-cash offer of many millions of dollars, when it is clear that the request is sincere, the response usually becomes thoughtful and, at times, very helpful.

Let's say that the buyer and seller have reached an impasse and cannot quite get to contract. There is nothing wrong in asking the seller's agent something like "Maybe you can help me. I know our clients want to get a deal done here, but we just cannot seem to get there. What do you realistically think is a way to close the gap that might work for both sides?"

Note the use of the word *realistically* and the phrase "what will work for both sides." This should, hopefully, avoid the snarky comeback of "Well, if the buyer just accepted the seller's last counteroffer, we would get to contract." But, of course, if you get that, there is no harm in chuckling and saying that you are serious in wondering if they have any ideas on how to break the logjam.

The little-discussed secret of real estate brokerage is that the agents often discuss ideas on what compromises they can each sell to their respective clients. Some agents have asked whether there is anything unethical about the agents essentially negotiating the deal behind the backs of their clients. The answer, with one caveat, is an absolute no!

Exploring how parties can reach an agreement or

resolve differences is exactly what agents should be doing. We would have far fewer real estate transactions if agents did not have these types of discussions on a regular basis. But there should be some limits to these discussions.

First, agents should clearly state that whatever agreements they think might work are still subject to the approval of their clients. They should avoid making statements like "I can definitely get my client to agree to that" unless the client has already indicated that a concession on that point is acceptable. This avoids you losing face with the other agent because you misjudged your client. It also avoids you pushing your client to accept an agreement they are uncomfortable with because you already agreed to it with the other agent.

Second, you should share with your client that you are having these discussions. Most clients will be grateful that the discussions are being had. However, if, for some reason, your client does not want these backchannel discussions to take place, you must respect your client's wishes and cease from having them.

Chapter 20

LEARN TO SIGNAL THE OTHER AGENT WHEN THINGS GET DICEY

As YOU START down the road of a negotiation, neither party quite knows where it will lead. Some buyers will pay substantially more for a property than they had planned, while some sellers might sell for less. Still others have unique needs, which, if they cannot be met, will make a deal a nonstarter. Buyers and sellers sometimes change their minds altogether. There can be dozens of issues that affect a buyer's decision to buy and a seller's decision to sell.

To a certain degree, receiving offers and counteroffers will let the other party know where the negotiation is heading. Unfortunately, in some instances, a client's hot-button issues that may prevent a deal from coming together are not clearly communicated. As we've mentioned, great negotiators always ask whether the other party has issues or needs that could affect the price or terms of the transaction. However, if one agent does not ask, the other agent should volunteer information if doing so will help prevent a transaction from falling apart.

There are many times in a negotiation where one of the parties may, unbeknownst to the other party, be at their wit's end and at a point of no return. As a great negotiator, the agent's role through communication is to signal to the other agent what those issues are or that the negotiation is about to hit a brick wall and possibly come to an end. While the agent could obviously be bluffing in giving these signals, the smart play here is to save these signals for real potential problems. Obviously, if the agent signals that the buyer has no ability to increase her offer and the buyer then increases it by $5,000, it destroys the agent's credibility.

Signaling is just another word for communicating. It usually starts with the phrase, "Hey, I just want to give you a head's up that . . ." The message is then whatever might derail the transaction. While signaling the other agent will not save deals that were not meant to be saved, they tend to prevent deals from falling apart for unknown reasons. This at least allows the other party the opportunity to make a rational decision on whether to try to save the transaction or let it die a natural death.

Of course, one should always get permission and discuss this strategy with their client before divulging sensitive information. Then, as you communicate or signal your client's position, do not forget to show empathy for the position of the other party. The following dialogue between two agents in the midst of a repair negotiation is an example of how an agent might signal the other agent that her client has reached a boiling point:

Seller's Agent: "I'm sorry, but my clients simply will not agree to replace the water heater just because the inspector says it is at the end of its useful life. It's working today, so they won't fix it."

Buyer's Agent: "Paula, I get it. But, here's the thing. My clients faced almost this exact situation with their last home. The seller on that transaction felt the same way your clients do. Unfortunately for my client, one week after closing, the water heater burst and flooded their basement. They not only had to replace the water heater but they also had to fix the hardwoods. As I'm sure you can appreciate, they are pretty gun-shy when it comes to water heaters. They simply aren't willing to take that risk again. Knowing that this is a particular sticking item for them, what can we do to help bridge the gap?"

There is no guarantee that the buyer's agent in this situation would change the mind of the seller, but she certainly made a more compelling argument than if she had said, "My clients won't agree otherwise." Now, presenting a solution along with the background information might be even better. It is as equally important to provide an "out" or a positive solution to allow the other party to meet your client where they want to be. In the foregoing example, perhaps the solution would be to present the story and suggest that the seller provide a home warranty instead of purchasing a new water heater. Solution-oriented thinking and a bit of personal truth might just make the difference between deal or no deal in this sort of situation.

Chapter 21

REPEATEDLY TELL THE LISTING AGENT WHY YOUR CLIENT LOVES THE HOUSE

SOME PEOPLE BELIEVE that knocking the house your client is trying to buy is a good way to justify a low offer to a seller. This strategy is grounded in the idea that a buyer will have greater leverage in a negotiation if they show the seller the reasons others would not want to buy the house at list price. While we agree that it is a good idea to have a sound basis for any offer you present on behalf of a client, we would caution against prefacing offers with negative commentary about the home. But if you are not knocking the house in any way, how do you get the seller to come down on their price? The answer is twofold.

First, repeatedly compliment the house and give the

sellers credit for making it great. You want the sellers to believe that the buyer loves the house more than any other buyer possibly could. Sellers want to sell their home to buyers who love it. This is why love letters were so common before there were fair housing concerns expressed about their use. Some sellers will even take less to sell to buyers who absolutely love their home.

The trick is to communicate how much the buyer loves the home without conveying desperation. This can be achieved by making it clear that the buyer made a thoughtful, business-minded offer, not a buy-it-at-any-cost offer. Also avoid statements like "My buyer said she absolutely must have this house." Instead, try saying something like "My buyer really loves the flow of the house. It is so warm and inviting. She thinks the sellers have done an outstanding job with it, and she is excited about the offer. I think you will agree that it is very reasonable based on comparable sales in the neighborhood."

Second, blame the buyer's budget, not the condition of the house, for not being able to offer more. This has to be done carefully so that the seller won't begin to think the buyer cannot afford to buy their home. Show the seller that the buyer is fully qualified and approved to buy the house at the price she is offering. But then say that your client's budget limits her to the price you have offered. Try saying something like "My buyer is very proactive and began working with her lender before we even started looking at homes. She has been fully prequalified up to this price. As I mentioned, she adores this home and is so impressed by what the sellers have done with it, but her last offer is really the most she can do right now. There just isn't any more leeway in her budget."

This type of comment should be made only after you get within striking distance of the list price. If you blame the buyer's budget too early, this strategy may backfire and leave the seller feeling that the price gap is just too great to overcome. But if you get within striking distance and have convinced the seller of the buyer's love for the house, the seller may make a larger price concession than they originally intended to sell the house to someone who loves it. You want the seller and the listing agent to be rooting for your client to get the house.

All of that said, there are certainly occasions where some negative aspect of the house sets it apart from comparable listings and sales in the vicinity. In those instances, it could be strategically beneficial to acknowledge the issue to the seller, but make sure to do so in a positive way. With this approach, telling the seller that there are some things that are not quite perfect about a property helps to justify the lower price the buyer wants to pay.

For example, a conversation between the listing agent and the buyer's agent might go like this:

Buyer's Agent: "My buyers really love the house. It appears to be very well-built and has good flow between rooms."

Seller's Agent: "Thank you. The sellers are really proud of it. They are the only owners of the house."

Buyer's Agent: "You can tell that the sellers have taken great care of this home. My buyers also liked the wonderful privacy the house affords."

Seller's Agent: "Yes, the house is situated on the lot in a way that maximizes the privacy."

Buyer's Agent: "The only concern my buyers have with the house is that the kitchen and bathrooms are a bit dated. The other homes we've seen at this price point have been fully updated. The buyer sees a ton of potential here and knows these things can all be renovated, but it will cost some real money to do so."

Seller's Agent: "True, but the buyers can do that over time to get the house looking exactly the way they want. In the meantime, they are still very functional."

Buyer's Agent: "The buyers are willing to increase the price they are offering, but their price will reflect that renovations will be needed."

Seller's Agent: "I understand. We will take a close look at your offer, and I will explain your concerns to the sellers."

The beauty of what the buyer's agent did here was that she constructively presented the positive aspects of the house that her clients appreciated without gushing over it and making the buyer sound desperate. She then presented her objection. Because she acknowledged the good with the bad, she sounded more credible and realistic. Her argument was more authentic than if she had simply said, "This house needs a ton of work, so your sellers will need to lower the price or my client just can't see a reason to move forward." A bit of tact can go a long way to getting what your client wants.

This bit of advice comes with a word of caution.

We briefly mentioned love letters above, and we would like to reiterate that we do not encourage their use. Love letters are notes that a buyer writes a seller begging them to accept their offer because of personal reasons. Perhaps it is because they have a new baby and they can see raising their family in the home in that particular neighborhood. It could also be that they have a handicapped family member, and the home has perfect accessibility.

These types of letters might pull at the heartstrings of the seller, but they also run the risk of creating fair housing issues if the seller decides to sell or not to sell based on an unlawful criterion. It is always best to keep any positive comments restricted to those that relate to the strictly physical parts of the home like layout and architecture. And by all means, never include a picture with an offer. If you are a listing broker, speak to the seller about the risks of accepting love letters, and with the seller's approval, include a comment in the listing that love letters will not be accepted or considered.

Finally, if you are representing the seller, anticipate what things a buyer might criticize about the home, and be prepared with responses. One highly respected agent we know bluntly says that the other word for a resale house is a used house, and that when you buy used, it is not going to be perfect. This "get over it, we aren't selling a new house" response often works for her. Another option is simply to tell the buyer's agent that those issues were factored into the original pricing of the house. Lastly, if the buyer's critique is based on a subjective issue, then politely point out that while you appreciate the buyer's position, their personal preference is unique to them and doesn't change the value of the property.

Chapter 22

EXPECT OCCASIONAL EXTREME BEHAVIOR FROM OTHER AGENTS

SOMETIMES, NO MATTER how friendly you are, the agent on the other side of the transaction will react to you or something you said negatively. After all, buyers and sellers aren't the only ones who have emotions that impact how they act. There are times in negotiations when the behavior of the other agent may be even more extreme than that of the parties. They may get angry or become hostile, argumentative, bullying, or distraught. They may call you names or question your ethics, honesty, and professionalism. What does this type of behavior mean and how should you react?

Anger and hostility are often an expression of one of

three things. First, and sometimes surprisingly, they can be used to try to achieve a goal where rational discussions have not succeeded. Many of us are socialized to avoid conflict and to calm an angry person. Knowing this, some people will consciously attempt to better their position simply by pitching a fit. Anger and hostility can also be used to intimidate an opponent into backing down from their position.

Second, anger isn't always used as a calculated weapon; sometimes it is simply an expression of frustration when things are not going the way we expect. If, for example, a listing agent has assured a client that their home is worth a particular price and the only offer the seller then gets is for a substantially lower price, the listing agent may become noticeably frustrated. Real estate is a business where we cannot always predict what a house will trade for, and there will always be surprises. If a client reacts poorly to such a surprise, they might lash out at their agent. Ultimately, an agent's reputation gets challenged when the unexpected occurs, so it isn't surprising when the unexpected is met with an emotionally charged response. An unexpected offer is almost like hearing "you were wrong" from the person making the offer. People tend to react poorly to such declarations.

Third, anger is an expression of outrage if a person feels that they have been mistreated. A hostile reaction to unethical behavior on the part of the other agent is a great example of anger resulting from a sense of outrage.

The trick to dealing with anger, whatever its cause, is to try very hard not to get caught up in it and to avoid emotional responses. This can often be difficult to do, particularly if the anger involves attacking your ethics, questioning your integrity, or leveling accusations that are unfounded. Sometimes, all the agent really needs is a bit of control. You can give that to the agent with your words.

So, for example, if you've made an offer that was lower than the listing agent and seller expected, and the response is anger, then put the ball back in the listing agent's court. Rationally tell the listing agent that you need help justifying a higher price to your buyer. Ask them to give you an explanation about why a particular comp should be ignored or given more weight than another. If you tell the agent that you are trying to help them get their expected price but you need their help, you are more likely to elicit a less emotional response.

When you see a conversation heading down an

anger-filled road, the best solution is to say to yourself (over and over again, if need be) that this is the time when the other side is using anger to try to achieve their goals. In such situations and to the extent possible, you want to disengage and avoid getting drawn into the fray in which you may say something you didn't intend. Evaluating calmly and silently why the other party is expressing anger is often a worthwhile distraction and sometimes educational in better understanding their perspective on the negotiation.

The reality about angry outbursts is that many truths are often said in anger that the other party can learn from if they are paying close attention. Of course, it is exceptionally hard for most of us not to respond when we are being yelled at or called names. Reasoning with a person who is acting irrationally is rarely successful. Encouraging the other agent to act professionally will rarely achieve a positive result either. Usually, it just makes the person even angrier. Sometimes, they just need some time to calm down. Disengaging can give them that time.

Since most conversations between agents are over the phone, or by email or text, it is easy enough to disengage by simply saying that you have another call coming in or are starting a meeting with another client and cannot continue the conversation.

If the other agent insists on a follow-up conversation, and it appears that its main purpose is for them to yell at you some more, it is okay to tell her to put her concerns in an email or text. Of course, it is more preferable to try to engage in a conversation and try to get the outstanding issues resolved. If things get really bad, it is appropriate to say that you will not participate in further conversations where the other agent is yelling. Of course, this may lead to a fight over whether the other person was yelling.

During the forced time-out, the agent who was yelled at should continue to evaluate why the other agent is angry. In many cases, there may have been a misunderstanding where the angry agent believed that the other agent did something underhanded or unethical. If that is the case, the agent who bore the brunt of the other agent's anger may want to send an email explaining exactly what happened. It may not change anything, but then again, it might.

One other suggestion is to invite the angry person to meet you for a cup of coffee at a location where there will be other people. Of course, the likelihood of her accepting is small. If she attends, there is also a chance that the conversation will devolve into an ugly scene. In many cases, however, the angry person is more likely to be on their best behavior in a public place, and the parties may actually talk through the issues and get to a better place. If nothing else works, having your broker call the other agent's broker might also be an option.

Chapter 23

BE CAREFUL
MAKING ULTIMATUMS

FOR BETTER or for worse, making an ultimatum is a great way to end a negotiation. There are times when communicating that you are done making concessions needs to occur, or the negotiation could be never-ending. However, an ultimatum should be used judiciously and should never be made unless the party making it is truly ready to walk away if her ultimatum is rejected.

If you are representing a client who has instructed you to issue an ultimatum on her behalf, it is important to discuss the risks of this course of action. Some people simply refuse to respond to ultimatums on principle. People who feel this way will often allow the negotiations to end in response to an ultimatum even if they would have been willing to make further concessions otherwise. Additionally, if you throw down the ultimatum gauntlet when you don't intend to follow through with the threat, you risk damaging your credibility with the other party, making further negotiations that much more difficult.

Unfortunately, some people don't care about the latter risk and use ultimatums as a negotiating tactic to extort concessions even though they have no intent of actually walking away from the transaction. They are betting that the person on the other side of the table will crumble in the face of the threat. If, instead, the other party calls their bluff and rejects the ultimatum, it leaves the person who made the ultimatum in a quandary. If they continue trying to negotiate, they end up with egg on their face, lose all credibility, and come across as desperate. It can actually create a situation where the party whose bluff was called ends up having to give away more than they would have otherwise had to if an ultimatum had not been made in the first instance. If that party does reach their true breaking point, it is likely their ultimatum won't be believed because they previously cried wolf.

For this reason, agents should discourage their clients from making false ultimatums. If the client is at all tentative about the finality of the transaction, the agent should encourage the party to make a counteroffer that is only nominally different than the last offer or counteroffer. This indicates that the party is close to the end in terms of making concessions without drawing hard lines in the sand.

If you do reach the point where you must issue an ultimatum, then try to do so with grace, not aggression. For example, if your seller client has reached a point where they are unwilling to continue to negotiate the sale, don't say, "My seller has told you what he will do. Take it or leave it." The attitude with which this ultimatum is delivered is more likely to turn off the other party than it is to get them to concede, which is the ultimate goal. Instead, say, "I appreciate that you've worked so hard to help bridge this gap; however, the sellers have made all the concessions they are willing to make. I'd love to see your buyer get this house, but unless they come up, my client has instructed me to end negotiations."

There are some buyers and sellers who hate to negotiate, evaluate the best price they can offer, make their final and best offer up front, and then stick with it. The challenge in being on the receiving end of this type of offer is determining whether this is truly their best offer. With this type of negotiator, a rejection of their offer results in them walking away from the transaction with a comment to get back in touch with them if anything changes. This at least leaves the door open in most cases to further discussions should the other side reconsider their offer.

Similarly, if you are representing the buyer on the receiving end of an ultimatum, and if they still really want the house after the seller has stopped negotiating, then be sure to keep an eye on the listing. If it doesn't sell within a few weeks, it is likely worth giving it another shot. Sometimes sellers just need a market reality check before they will continue negotiating.

Chapter 24

DON'T SPLIT THE DIFFERENCE UNLESS IT IS LOGICAL TO DO SO

SPLITTING THE DIFFERENCE in a real estate negotiation is a common way to resolve differences when there is sound logic behind each party's position. Each party gives up something, you meet in the middle, and there is an equitable resolution to the issue. While that may sound good, the problem with splitting the difference is that the parties to negotiations have learned to game the system. They take more extreme positions than are reasonable so that when the difference is then split, it will create a favorable advantage for them.

If you are the recipient of an offer to split the difference, first evaluate it to determine if the end result would actually result in a fair compromise. To do that, you cannot simply consider where each party currently stands in the negotiation. You also have to consider the reasonableness of the parties' respective starting positions in light of the current market in the area where the property is, and you have to evaluate the concessions each has already made or not made, as the case may be.

Let's look at the following example to better understand this. A seller's house has recently appraised for $725,000, and the house is listed for $750,000. A buyer offers $600,000 for the house. The seller counters at the full listing price of $750,000. The buyer's agent suggests that the parties split the difference. This would result in the house selling at $675,000. Depending on the state of the real estate market, this may or may not be a fair price for the property. In an extreme seller's market or a balanced market, it would be a very low price to accept. In an extreme buyer's market, $50,000 under the appraised price may or may not be right.

The point is that without an analysis of where the middle gets you in splitting the difference, the approach is arbitrary and may result in compromise that makes little sense.

Usually, you can see based on the size of each party's concessions where the negotiation will end up. If the seller is reducing the sales price by $10,000 for each increase in the offering price by the buyer of $20,000, it is easy to play this out a few rounds to see where the parties will ultimately end up in terms of a sales price. This is a variation on splitting the difference, but agents should always be thinking several rounds ahead to see where the negotiation is going. If a party doesn't like where things are heading, they should immediately change the reductions or increases in their offers to something that will produce a more favorable result.

Chapter 25

WIN-WIN NEGOTIATIONS ARE LARGELY A MYTH

As WE'VE DISCUSSED, negotiations always take place in the context of the market in which the buyer and seller find themselves. When the parties come to the table with perfectly equal negotiating power, the negotiation should result in transactions that create a win-win situation for both parties. But when the market favors one party or the other, which is commonly the case, rarely does the negotiation result in what would widely be considered a win-win scenario.

For example, in an extreme seller's market, there are likely going to be multiple buyers making offers on the same property. The "winning" buyer will probably have to pay over list price to purchase the property. When it comes time to resell the property, the buyer might not be able to get out what they put into the purchase. Is that really a win-win negotiation? Similarly, in an extreme buyer's market, the seller is going to be lucky to receive any offers. If one is made, it will be at the lowest possible price because, frankly, if the seller does not accept the buyer's offer, it is unclear whether or when another offer will be received. In this type of market, the seller may end up having to bring cash to the closing. Does this result in what could fairly be descried as a win-win negotiation? The answer is obviously not.

Even in relatively balanced markets, the parties rarely have perfectly equal bargaining leverage. Be it the market or the parties' personal situations, somebody will always want to sell more than another party wants to purchase or vice versa. As a result, agents would do well not to talk about a win-win negotiation as a goal.

An agent's job isn't to negotiate a win-win deal where the buyer and seller benefit equally from the transaction. Instead, an agent has to redefine what "winning" means in the context of the current market. Success might mean something different in each transaction an agent closes. If the parties were able to deal fairly and honestly by doing the things that they said they were going to do, then there is likely going to be a good result. In truth, that is about as much as any agent can hope to achieve. If the market favors one party or the other, pushing for the best deal possible for that party is part of the agent's job.

At the end of the day, the true measure of whether or not a real estate transaction was a win-win is the ultimate happiness of the respective parties. Even if the deal seems to favor one party over the other on paper, if both buyer and seller are happy with the outcome, then that is a true success.

Chapter 26

LEAVING ROOM TO NEGOTIATE CONCESSIONS

LEAVING ROOM to make concessions is a cardinal rule in many types of business negotiations; however, it is not always appropriate in a negotiation to buy or sell a house. With real estate negotiations, leaving room to negotiate can actually result in final terms that are less favorable to your client than they would have been otherwise. The longer a house sits on the market, for example, the harder it is to sell at a great price. Therefore, pricing a house where it will sell quickly relative to the market should always be a goal.

Similarly, where there is a scarcity of quality housing, a buyer needs to come to the table with their strongest offer. With so much competition, the buyer does not

177

have the luxury of coming in with a low offer where they have room to negotiate. Likewise, in an extreme buyer's market, a seller might be better served by listing the home for the lowest price they are willing to accept rather than listing it too high and receiving no offers at all.

An agent also needs to consider their client's personal circumstances. For example, perhaps your seller client has taken a new job out of state, and they need to move as quickly as possible. In that case, it might be wise to forgo leaving room to negotiate. You have to determine what matters most to that particular seller: the speed of the sale or the purchase price. Naturally, most people would love to have their cake and eat it too. The seller in this scenario might value time and money equally. Why wouldn't they want to sell for as much money as possible as quickly as possible? But what does "quickly" mean to this seller, and what would they think was a good price? Quickly might mean something different to you than it does to your client, so ask the question.

If you represented this seller, then your job would have been to set reasonable expectations about the average time on market in that area and average price points for similar homes in the area. Let's say the average time on market is thirty days, and when your seller said they wanted to move quickly, they were thinking sixty days or less. If that were the case, perhaps they could be a bit more aggressive with pricing. As long as you have done your due diligence and listened to what matters to your client, you can help your client make this sort of evaluation.

So when does it make sense to leave room to negotiate? For those who subscribe to the "never accept the first offer" mentality, they might be more inclined to pad their list price a bit to accommodate that strategy. Further, in a relatively balanced market, there is somewhat of an expectation that people are likely to enter the negotiation with room to negotiate. Your client would need to follow suit so that they are able to play the same negotiating game. If there is room to negotiate, then a seller (or buyer) can make concessions to communicate that they are reasonable. That, in turn, can set the tone for the negotiation going forward.

If it does make sense to leave room to negotiate, you then have to determine what that looks like. Unfortunately, there is no magic formula to leaving room to negotiate. There is no negotiating rule of thumb that says 3 percent, 5 percent, or some other amount is the winning margin of negotiating room that is best. The reason for that is because the best negotiators do not use obvious strategies. They mix things up a bit. You have to look at the broader picture to figure out the appropriate margin in your particular case.

For example, if your buyer wants to make a low offer to leave themselves room to negotiate, you might ask questions such as these:

1. What is the average ratio of sales price to list price in your area?

2. Is the list price reasonable?

3. How long has the property been on the market versus the average time on market in your area?

4. Have there been other offers?

5. Does the property have unique features that are difficult to find in your area?

6. Does the seller live in the home, and if so, for how long?

7. Has the seller renovated the home?

8. Are there any special circumstances on the buyer's or seller's side of the transaction?

LEAVING ROOM TO NEGOTIATE CONCESSIONS

To understand the importance of these questions, we can look at them one by one. First, what is the average ratio of sales price to list price in your area? Perhaps the homes in your area typically sell for 96 percent of the list price. This tells you that sellers in your market on average are leaving themselves room to negotiate. If this particular seller has done so, then that is a great indication that they are open to negotiating. So how do you determine if this seller has left 4 percent negotiating room? You ask the second question.

Is the list price reasonable? If you have done your homework, which hopefully you have, then you should already have a good idea of what sales price is reasonable. Compare that to the actual list price. Are they the same? If not, what is the delta? If the seller is asking more than 4 percent (the average sales to list price ratio in the area) above what you believe is reasonable, then this might indicate that the seller has unreasonable expectations. If the sales price is right around 4 percent over the reasonable price, then you know that the seller and/or their agent also know the market and are probably willing to negotiate. If they have priced it right at the price you believe is reasonable, then that might communicate that they are serious, knowledgeable sellers who perhaps don't want to mess around. If the home is underpriced, that might tell you that the seller is highly motivated or that they haven't done their research. Whatever the case, by asking yourself these questions, you might get clues about what to offer.

Third, ask how long the home has been on the market in relation to average time on market in the area. Say, for example, homes in your area are typically on the market for thirty days, and this particular property has already been on the market for twenty-five days. What might this mean? Well, it could mean that the seller is unreasonable. As we have just learned, you can also look at the list price to get a clue about that. It might also mean that there is something about the home that is making it less desirable than other homes in the area. Whatever the cause, the result is likely that the seller, assuming they actually want to sell, is getting a bit nervous. They might be more open to negotiating because the listing is getting stale. Note that the longer a home sits on the market, the greater pressure an agent feels to get it sold. This means you might be able to come in lower than you would if the property had been on the market for only two days.

Next, ask if there have been any other offers.

Sometimes this information is difficult to get. Agents are not always willing to divulge too much unless they think the answer is one that will create a sense of urgency in the buyer. You might also look at the listing history to see if the home has been under contract previously. A home that has been listed for a while with no offers might be more susceptible to a lower offer. The reverse is also true. If a home has had a lot of offers, then it is likely best to submit a stronger offer from the start.

Next, you can ask if the property has unique or novel features that are difficult to find. For example, perhaps your buyer is looking for a home with a detached garage, which are difficult to find in their search area. If you find a home that has one, it might be smarter to proceed with a stronger offer to ensure the buyer does not miss out.

Another important question to ask is whether or not the seller lives in the home, and if so, for how long. As we have discussed in previous chapters, emotion often plays a significant role in a buyer's or seller's negotiations. A seller who has lived in the home for many years may have a personal connection to it. There could also be a sense of pride associated with the home. They may even see the home as a reflection of who they are as a person. If that is the case, a lowball offer might be insulting. Conversely, an investor or somebody who has lived in the home for only a short time might be less emotionally connected to the transaction, which in turn might give a buyer more flexibility with their offer.

When determining how much room to leave for negotiating, you should also consider whether or not the seller has made significant improvements to the home. The answer to this question can be important for two reasons. First, if a seller has spent a lot of money on the property, they may be less willing to negotiate because they are trying to recoup those expenditures. Second, a seller who has renovated a home might see an offer as a judgment of their work. If an offer is too low, the seller might see that as a critique and feel insulted.

Finally, it is always important to ask if there are any special circumstances for a buyer or a seller. Asking the other agent why a seller decided to sell, for example, could reveal information that is relevant. For example, perhaps it is an estate sale or maybe there is a divorce. If the other agent is willing to give you information, that might be useful information when deciding what to offer.

These are just some of the questions you might want

to ask when determining whether or not to leave room to negotiate, and if so, how much room to leave. There are many others that might be appropriate in a given situation. These questions are important whether you are setting the list price or presenting an offer. What a smart negotiator will remember is that every action you make in a negotiation communicates something about your client and about you. It is likely that the person on the other side will make correct and incorrect assumptions about you based on that offer or listing price, so be strategic. Ask a lot of questions, and try to put yourself in the shoes of the party on the other side of the negotiating table.

Chapter 27

QUID PRO QUOS

SOME EXPERT NEGOTIATORS will tell you that you should never give anything away in a negotiation without getting something in return. In Latin, this is called a quid pro quo. While that strategy may work well in business or legal negotiations, it tends to be less successful at certain phases of negotiations for the purchase and sale of a house. Part of becoming an expert agent negotiator is anticipating issues, thinking strategically, and helping your client reset expectations when it comes to quid pro quos.

A real estate negotiation over the purchase and sale of a house can often be a long-drawn-out affair. It starts with the first phone call to the seller's agent and does not end until the parties are sitting at the closing table, sometimes not even then. Just because the parties have signed a contract does not mean that the transaction will actually close. It's not over until it's over, as they say. Haggling over the major terms and getting the initial agreement bound is only phase one.

Phase two comes after the contract is signed. Residential real estate contracts generally have at least one or more contingencies. These contingencies represent questions, the answers to which are pivotal in determining whether or not a transaction actually closes. Will the buyer be able to get financing by a given date? Will the property appraise for the purchase price? Will an inspection reveal any defects with the property? Will title to the property be clear? Will the buyer's current home sell in time?

There are an unlimited number of questions that might matter to the parties in any given transaction. Part of an agent's job is anticipating outcomes and preparing for them. Then there are the issues that arise unexpectedly such as the loss of a job, a serious illness, a tree limb that falls and damages the roof, or a pipe that bursts inside the home. One party might need to ask for a favor and a bit of grace in such a circumstance. Building goodwill with the other party whenever the opportunity presents itself in a transaction can be the glue that prevents a deal from falling apart if the expected, or unexpected, comes to pass.

During the first phase of offers and counteroffers, trading concessions is commonplace. In fact, exchanging concessions in these early stages of a negotiation can actually go a long way to structuring a deal that meets the needs of both parties. But don't forget that you're playing a long game. There will most likely be a second phase of negotiations where you will want something from the other party or where they will want something from you. For that reason, making a concession that isn't reciprocated during this first phase can actually be a smart strategy. Being flexible and generous establishes you as a reasonable person and gives you ammunition you will likely need in phase two.

Let's say that buyer's agent, Bob, and seller's agent, Sally, have been helping the parties negotiate the sale of a condo. Sally tells Bob that the seller will agree to pay the requested $5,000 toward the buyer's closing costs, but only if the buyer allows the seller to stay in the condo rent free for one week after closing. Bob is able to get his clients to agree. By exchanging concessions, the parties each obtain things that matter to them in the transaction. This works because each party has something the other party wants, and the agents understand what is important to the parties.

Now let's say that the buyer also wanted the seller to purchase a home warranty for them. The seller's first instinct might be to say no, but it is Sally's job to look at the situation strategically and to help her client weigh the benefits of being cooperative. The following interaction between Sally and her seller shows how their conversation might look.

> **Sally:** "Bob just called and said his buyer is requesting that you buy them a $600 home warranty. If you agree to this last thing, then they will sign the contract."
>
> **Seller:** "What do I get in return?"
>
> **Sally:** "They aren't offering anything additional at this point, but we've come a long way in this negotiation. You're already getting more for the home than you anticipated, and they are allowing you to stay in the home after closing. I think you should really consider accepting this final term so that we can finalize this deal."
>
> **Seller:** "If they want a $600 home warranty, then

I want to be able to stay in the house for an extra week after closing. I could use that extra time."

Sally: "I will ask for the extra week if that is what you would like me to do. However, I think it might actually benefit you to agree to this without changing any other terms."

Seller: "How so?"

Sally: "The buyer has a ten-day inspection period. Chances are high that an inspector will find something wrong. That's what they're paid to do. Agreeing to the home warranty now might help us when it comes time to negotiating repairs."

Seller: "Okay, but if I just give in on this, they'll think they can push me around about repairs too. I can't allow that."

Sally: "Remember, you don't have to agree to do any repairs regardless of what the buyer thinks. Agreeing to buy a home warranty will signal to the buyer that you're being reasonable. I'll make sure to tell Bob how much you appreciate the buyer working through these issues with us to plant that seed. I'll even suggest that Bob remind his clients how generous you've been when it comes time to ask for repairs. I've seen buyers go easy on the repair requests when the sellers have shown good faith. It builds trust and sets potentially nervous buyers at ease."

Seller: "I don't know. Six hundred dollars is a lot, and there is no guarantee that the buyer will go easy on the repair list."

Sally: "I get it. But if they do ask for a lot of repairs, we can remind them that the home warranty will cover a lot of issues. We know that the water heater is at the end of its useful life and has begun rusting. They are likely to ask for you to replace it. A home warranty is certainly less expensive than a new water heater. I really think you have more to gain by agreeing to the home warranty than you do from staying in the house an extra week. You've already said that a week is really all you need."

This exchange shows that by forgoing the tit-for-tat mentality, Sally set the seller up to have an advantage in the inevitable repair negotiation to come. There was also the added benefit of establishing trust with a potentially anxious buyer and positioning the seller to be in a good place should anything unexpected occur prior to settlement.

Sally did something else in her exchange with the seller that all agents should consider when addressing requests from the opposing party. She helped the seller weigh the value of agreeing to the request against the value of what was to be gained by seeking a quid pro quo. In this case, the value of establishing goodwill for upcoming repair negotiations arguably outweighed the benefit of spending an extra week in the home after completion of the sale.

Some requests or favors are so small that saying yes is a no-brainer. Agreeing to extend a deadline by a day, for example, is arguably a concession that might cost your client nothing. If agreeing costs your client very little, then they generally always have more to gain by showing cooperation than they do by being difficult. Doing favors freely and willingly to a point shows that one has acted beyond every measure of reasonableness. It is like buying an insurance policy to insure that the transaction will close.

Of course, in doing such favors, it is perfectly okay for the parties to remind each other that they are doing favors that they are not obligated to do, and that they expect the favor will be reciprocated if the need arises. If there is a minor concession that one party wants to request, that is okay too so long as it does not look like a price will need to be paid for every favor that is requested.

There will also be times when party A will do a favor for party B and then party B refuses to reciprocate when party A needs a favor. While this can be frustrating, most agents will tell you that in the course of many real estate transactions, both sides will need a favor. Therefore, payback can be hell when one side refuses to grant a favor but then needs one later in the transaction.

Chapter 28

DON'T BARGAIN AGAINST YOURSELF

WE ALREADY DISCUSSED the value of patience and the power of creating a sense of urgency in your negotiations. Now that we have an understanding of how those concepts can be used offensively, we have to look at how to defend against them. To do this, let's explore one of the biggest dangers a party might face in a negotiation where the other party is strategically creating leverage. That danger is the tendency to bargain against oneself in response to pressure, and, generally, it should be avoided.

Looking at the idea of bargaining against oneself superficially, it seems like an obvious no-no. Why would anybody ever make a conscious choice to worsen their position in a negotiation? The problem is that people do not always recognize that they are doing it. Here is an example of what this might look like.

Paul and Paula, your buyer clients and dear friends, have found the house of their dreams listed for $500,000, but the seller's agent has informed you that he is expecting several offers in the coming days. Having created this sense of urgency, the seller is already establishing leverage. You talk to Paul and Paula about coming in with their strongest offer, so they ask you to submit a full-price offer on their behalf.

The next day, you still haven't heard from the listing agent. Your clients are calling and texting you every hour on the hour to see if you've heard from the seller. Evidently, they have not read this book and do not understand the value of patience. Tensions are definitely high. You talk to them about being patient, but they start to worry that every minute they don't hear from the seller increases the probability that the seller will receive a higher offer. You call the listing agent to find out the status, but you're given a noncommittal response about the seller being busy. You, too, now start to suspect that the seller is stalling intentionally. When you tell this to Paul and Paula, they decide that they need to submit a new offer to the seller, but this time, it will be one the seller cannot refuse. Even though you told them to go in with their highest and best offer from the get-go, your buyer clients are willing to stretch beyond their comfort zone and offer $545,000 to seal the deal.

And voila, Paul and Paula have just bargained against themselves. Now, it is certainly possible that this tactic will pay off, and Paul and Paula will get the house of their dreams. If they are happy with that result, then no harm, no foul. Chances are, however, that Paul and Paula might start to have buyer's remorse because they paid more than they wanted to pay for the house. It would be natural for them to wonder if they could have gotten the house for less if they had just waited. Were there ever any competing offers? Did they get outplayed by an agent who was a better negotiator? In a business that is so driven by relationships and referrals, being outplayed ends up being a bad result for you and your buyers, not to mention your friendship.

How might this have played out differently? The buyers could have been more patient. When the seller did not respond to their initial offer, the buyers' agent could have encouraged the buyers to start to look for a different house and could have communicated that to the seller's agent. If the seller's agent was stalling to see if the buyers could be spooked into making a higher offer, this would have called the listing agent's bluff and shifted the leverage back to the buyer. After all, the buyers could now go elsewhere, and the seller may have lost some very qualified buyers. If it wasn't a bluff, then a bit of patience may have saved the buyer money.

Let's look at another example of how a strong negotiator might try to get you to bargain against yourself to your detriment. Revisiting Paul and Paula's transaction, they are now happily under contract but then receive the appraisal from their lender, and the house appraises for only $490,000. Paul and Paula can bring cash to pay the gap between the appraised value and the purchase price, but fortunately, you negotiated an appraisal contingency for them. If the seller won't reduce the sales price to the appraised value, then Paul and Paula can terminate the agreement without penalty.

You send an amendment asking the seller to reduce the sales price and a copy of the appraisal to the listing agent. The agent discusses it with their client and comes back to you with the following statement: "My sellers received other offers, so they have said they aren't going to come down on the purchase price. If you can get your clients to submit a new amendment with a higher purchase price, I might be able to get my seller to consider it."

Notice that the agent didn't tell you how low the seller would go and didn't commit the seller to any particular deal. Unfortunately, Paul and Paula showed their cards to the seller when they voluntarily increased their original offer to buy the house. The seller knows that Paul and Paula are excited and really want the house. The listing agent has shifted the leverage the buyer gained with the appraisal contingency back to the seller. If your buyer is willing to submit a new amendment, then the listing agent will have successfully narrowed the negotiation playing field to the seller's advantage.

Paul and Paula now have to decide what purchase price to propose in the new amendment. They don't have a concept of how far the seller is willing to go, so they have to guess. Ultimately, your buyers offer a new amendment with a purchase price of $515,000. You submit the new amendment, and now the negotiations begin. The seller will likely counter because she knows the buyer is open to negotiating. After a bit of back-and-forth, the parties agree to meet roughly in the middle with a sales price of $530,000.

Psychologically speaking, most people accept meeting in the middle as a fair resolution to a dispute, but in this case, the seller actually won the negotiation, if you're keeping score at least. If the parties had truly met in the middle, then the purchase price would have been $297,500. By getting the buyers to bargain against themselves, the listing agent was able to shift the buyer's perception of where the middle was.

A smart agent would have identified the request to submit a new amendment as a signal that the seller was willing to negotiate a reduction in the sales price. She would then tell the seller's agent that if the sellers would like the buyers to consider an alternate sales price, then the seller should present an amendment. Most sellers who have shown a willingness to negotiate will agree. If they don't agree, then the buyer can consider if they are willing to take the risk of negotiating against themselves.

One thing that most agents understand and most buyers do not is that there is usually another good house coming along, even if the buyer misses out on the first one she falls in love with. The extreme seller's market of the early 2020s was one of the few times in history that this well-accepted rule broke down. However, in a normal market, if buyers can be educated on this principle, they are usually more patient and more willing not to bid against themselves when that temptation presents itself.

Chapter 29

GET THE DETAILS
IN WRITING

THERE ARE MANY TIMES in negotiations when the parties seemingly agree on the terms of a deal only to have things fall apart when they try to reduce the supposed agreement to writing. This can happen for several reasons.

First, messages sometimes get garbled in communications from the clients to their agents. When the agent presents what she thought was the agreement, the client responds with those terrible words, "This isn't what I agreed to." Second, clients change their minds and often feel free to do so until they have signed on the dotted line. Sometimes, the client will use the lack of a written agreement as an excuse to remember verbal agreements differently than what actually was the agreement.

Buyers and sellers do not always articulate their preferences clearly to their agents because they are often unfamiliar with the process. Sometimes, however, it is the agent who is not listening carefully to what their client is saying. An agent should always slow down to make sure they both clearly articulate details when speaking to their clients and listen carefully to what their client is saying. It can be helpful to consider the level of experience your client has when discussing contract terms. While it goes without saying that a first-time homebuyer is going to need a more thorough explanation than a seasoned investor who buys and sells homes regularly, things that seem obvious to you may not be obvious to your client.

Whether a miscommunication is the result of a client who doesn't communicate clearly or an agent who doesn't listen carefully, the end result is the same. The agent who meant to communicate and negotiate on their client's behalf doesn't have a good foundation for doing so.

This garbled message between an agent and their client can then get further distorted as it is shared. You've likely played the telephone game. One person whispers something into the ear of the person next to them. That person then whispers the same message to the person next to them. This pattern continues down the line until the last person to receive the message recites it to the group. What makes the game fun is that the final message is usually some convoluted phrase that makes no sense and doesn't even resemble what the first person said. Unfortunately, it is not as much fun when a miscommunication gets in the way of real estate negotiations. The original message might get lost in translation and end up killing the deal. If nothing else, key details might be omitted. It isn't until one side or the other reduces the agreement to writing that the issue is discovered.

The solution to these problems is always to try to get agreements reduced to writing as quickly as possible. The challenge with this approach is that writing things down takes time, and many agents are reluctant to invest that time until they know they have a deal. The solution, of course, is to take the time even though it might never pay off. In the long term, you will save more time because you did things correctly up front.

Written terms can not only help keep the negotiating parties on the same page but can also be easier for some people to understand. As we've mentioned several times in this book, buying a home is one of the biggest investments a person makes in their life. They might feel comfort in having an agent who is willing to take the time to put things in writing to make sure they understand everything clearly. That sort of patience will not only go a long way to getting the deal closed but might also help you earn loyal clients and referrals in the future.

One approach is to write down the bullet points of an agreement and try to get confirmation that everyone is on the same page. Of course, even though this is an important approach that can help agents confirm their respective understandings of an agreement, it is not binding until it has been signed off on by the parties. Therefore, there is really no shortcut to writing down the agreement as quickly as possible and getting the parties to sign it.

In some states, agents can prepare a letter of intent, but they cannot make the actual contract or amendments to that contract. In other states, agents have the legal right to complete standard form contracts and draft special stipulations thereto. Just because they can, however, does not mean they should. An agent should always read an agreement before drafting any additional stipulations.

One of the biggest mistakes agents make when using preprinted contracts is to add an extra provision that repeats language that is already in the boilerplate language of the agreement. In doing so, an agent runs the risk of narrowing the rights of their client by writing the provision unclearly. These sorts of unnecessary stipulations might also communicate to the other side that you and/or your client are going to be difficult throughout the transaction. That is not the tone to set if you want a successful negotiation. In states where agents can prepare the contract, it is equally important to ask yourself the following questions in drafting contract provisions.

- WHO is going to do something?

- WHEN are they going to do it?

- HOW are they going to do it?

- WHAT are they going to do? Is what they are doing conditional, and if so, on what?

- WHAT happens if they don't do what they are supposed to do?

- IF the work can be unwarranted, is some type of warranty going to be issued?

For example, let's say that there is a leak into a finished

basement, and the seller has agreed to hire a professional waterproofing company to waterproof the basement wall. Language addressing this might state as follows:

The seller shall, at seller's sole expense, hire a professional waterproofing company [WHO is going to do something] to waterproof the rear basement wall beneath the kitchen of the house on the property [WHAT they are going to do]. Such work is to be completed prior to closing [WHEN the work is going to be performed] by excavating the wall to the full depth of the foundation wall, then installing a waterproof coating on membrane topped by damage panels to carry away water [HOW the work is going to be done]. Seller shall also perform such other work as is necessary to allow the waterproofing company to issue a sure (5) year warranty against further leaking [The Warranty] which provides that in the event of further leaks, the company will perform all additional work and supply all additional material to waterproof the walls against further leaks.

Taking the time to carefully draft agreements prevents parties from trying to get out of their obligations later by misconstruing poorly drafted provisions.

The other challenge in this area is getting the client to read and understand what has been written. Clients are notorious for skimming the fine print or relying on your explanation of the same. Encouraging clients to read everything they are signing carefully (and not just putting initials on an e-sign document) ensures that they really understand the agreement.

Finally, remember that the general rule in most every state is that no agreements are going to be enforceable until they have been reduced to writing and signed by the parties. This alone is why getting things in writing is so important.

Chapter 30

RESPONDING TO OBJECTIONS

ONE OF THE WAYS great negotiators succeed is by anticipating what objections will be made to particular positions and preparing ready responses to each objection. In essence, it is about learning to play a mental game in advance of a negotiation: "If she says *this*, I will respond by saying *this*." The more you can anticipate each successive round of the negotiation with points and counterpoints, the more successful you will be in negotiating favorable outcomes.

How many times have you had a negotiation not go well where afterward you wanted to kick yourself for not responding with something perfect because you only thought of it later? If you can be mentally disciplined enough to think through objections in advance, you will have fewer of those moments.

So, how exactly do you anticipate objections? It is mostly about learning to walk in another person's shoes. As a listing or buyer's agent, it requires you to see both the pluses and minuses of every piece of property with which you are involved. If you are a listing agent, it requires you to ask on each of your listings the following questions:

1. If I were representing the buyer, how would I argue for a lower price?

2. What are the negatives about the house, the property, the neighborhood, and the broader community?

You can then start to think about your response to each of those objections. Playing this game requires you to be brutally honest in identifying the faults with the properties you are listing.

So, for example, a friend recently bought a lake house where all of the properties in the neighborhood were on the side of a steep hill and were all, therefore, below the grade of the street. It is normally harder to sell houses below street grade, and our friend made that argument to support a lower price. The listing agent had obviously anticipated this objection and was ready with three responses, all of which were nicely articulated. First, she said, while that rule is generally true, it does not apply to lake properties where so many of them are on hills sloping toward the lake. Second, by moving the house farther down the hill toward the lake, the walk to the lake is much shorter. As she emphasized, you wouldn't want the house to be at the top of the hill and have a longer walk to the lake. Finally, she pointed out that all of the houses in the neighborhood were like this and that this was simply the standard for the neighborhood. Our friend was convinced. What, of course, was not said by the listing agent was that there were other neighborhoods that were not on a hill where none of the houses were below grade. Naturally, these houses were more expensive.

While you may be able to train yourself to anticipate the objections you will encounter in a negotiation, how you express those counterpoints is just as important as the points themselves. What you never want to do is to win the argument but lose the transaction.

It is always wise to communicate with kindness, prefacing your response with an acknowledgment that you hear and understand the point she is making and even stating, when appropriate, "That is a good point." It also helps if the agent communicates that the buyer is sincerely interested in the property at the same time the buyer agent is negotiating price and terms.

While achieving success in the negotiation is certainly important, when that does not happen—as will certainly be the case in some negotiations—the disappointment is usually tempered by being treated with courtesy and respect by the other agent.

Sometimes, objections made by the other agent will so hit the bull's-eye there will be little or no way to counter them. Usually, in such situations, it makes the most sense to acknowledge the point but not to respond to it. Alternatively, you can say that your client factored in that issue when they set a price for the property.

Also, as we emphasized earlier, negotiations do not have to be fair. When it comes to buying or selling real estate, parties are entitled to be as arbitrary as they want to be. Being arbitrary tends to resist appeals to reason. No one can be forced to buy or sell a house. And if a buyer wants to buy the house at that point in time, the buyer may well have to agree to terms that are undesirable to them. The same is true in reverse for sellers.

RESPONDING TO OBJECTIONS

Sometimes, in a negotiation, simply saying something like the following is the only thing you can do: "You make some excellent points, but the seller is just not going to go below their price at this time." Or you might say, "That's a great point, and the seller factored that in when she set her price."

Chapter 31

LEARN HOW TO USE TEXTING AND EMAIL CORRECTLY

MOST COMMUNICATIONS between agents these days are, sadly, by texting and email. Can you have meaningful negotiations with so few words actually exchanged between the parties? The answer, of course, is yes, but you need to be careful in how you do it.

The challenge is that there is only so much you can say in a text or email. You can give someone the bottom line in a text but not much context. The nuances of verbal communication with its changes in tone, sighs, pauses, and general ability to convey emotion are generally lost in texts and emails. So, a text or email is good when you are communicating agreement with the other party. Saying, "My client accepts your last counteroffer. I will send you the signed counter shortly" works fine other than it is not signed by the client and is thus unenforceable. Still, it quickly and easily communicates that the parties are in agreement.

Texts and emails are not as good where there is a need to explain the position of a party. So, can you text, "My client will only go to $562,000. They will not go to the $591,000 you asked for in your last counter"? Yes, you can do this, but with no context, the message may come across as too blunt, and, of course, the rationale for the counter is not given. While you can attempt to explain the rationale for the counteroffer in a long email, it will not be anywhere near as effective as a telephone conversation. More importantly, since people tend to be more direct and, at times, harsher in email and text communications, you may get a response that could cause the transaction to fall apart when this may not have happened in a phone call.

When explanations need to be given, it is better to call the other agent or text or email something like "My client is willing to go up on their last offer. Call me so I can explain." This is a bit of a teaser email or text. It tells the other agent that progress is being made but does not state the degree of that progress. If the other agent calls, you can tell her that your client will only go to $562,000 but also explain why that is the case. This at least gives you a chance to contextualize your client's position and give the other agent something to pass on to the sellers. You are also more likely to gain useful insights about the other party when you take the time to have an actual conversation with the other agent.

The increasing use of texting and emails in real estate negotiations is likely because of three reasons. First, it is a way for agents to avoid the potential for conflict in verbal communications. If this describes you, remember that you are being paid to be the intermediary and advocate where such conversations come with the turf. Remember also that you represent your client far more effectively through verbal communications. Second, they are used in certain extreme real estate markets where there is little need for agents to do much negotiation. As a result, they can quickly get out of practice. Third, emails and texts are fast. You are less likely to get pulled into lengthy conversations, and you can respond in your own time. While many of our negotiations will continue to involve email and text communications, learning when and when not to negotiate by text and email will make you more successful.

Chapter 32

NEGOTIATING TOWARD A MORE PRECISE PRICE

WHEN PARTIES NEGOTIATE using large round numbers, it is often an indication that they have not yet gotten close to the final number at which they can buy or sell a property. So, for example, if the buyer is increasing offers in increments of $10,000 and the seller is reducing the sales price in similar increments, it is often a signal that the parties are not yet at their final number.

When a party starts to negotiate using precise numbers, it signals that they are getting close to the final price. So, for example, if a buyer increases her offer by $3,675 after several rounds of negotiation, it comes across as if a lot of thought has been put into that particular offer, and the buyer is offering about as much as she can.

DONE DEAL

This might be particularly true if the newly offered price isn't precisely in the middle between the previously offered prices. Using a price that hasn't been rounded up to the nearest $500 or $10,000 signals that the party is close to the end—whether they truly are or not. As a result, your client may get a better price than they might have otherwise achieved.

Now, of course, if the seller makes one counteroffer and the buyer comes back at $576,837.50, the seller is unlikely to be convinced that the buyer is putting their last nickel into the deal. Including cents in the precise offer goes a bit too far. It can also be off-putting. For example, an agent shared a story with us about a seller that had been, in her words, "unnecessarily difficult." After a rough inspection, the parties decided to reduce the sales price in lieu of repairs. They haggled back and forth trying to agree on the ultimate sales price before the seller sent his "best and final" offer of $325,223.45. The buyer was so annoyed that the seller was quite literally nickeling and diming her that she walked away just on principle. Whether the seller was truly crunching numbers or playing a negotiating game, the end result was that the overly precise figure backfired. Had he

222

simply offered $325,225.00, she might have gone for it.

The moral of the story is that after several rounds of negotiations, a precise offer, but not too precise, sends a signal that the party has reached or is close to reaching their limit. It is a good tactic to remember. A precise number might also help a buyer in a multiple-offer situation. For example, if a buyer is willing to go up to an offer price of $100,000 but assumes that others might as well, an offer of $100,250 might make the difference between being the best or second-best offer.

In addition to considering precise offers, an agent should look at the increments of price concessions being made by each party to find a pattern that might communicate more about the opposing party's final position. As previously discussed, the relative size of the monetary concessions that each side makes has always been a sign of where a negotiation is heading. If the buyer is increasing the price that she will pay for a property by $25,000 in each round of offers and counteroffers, and the seller is only decreasing the sales price by $5,000 in each round, the ultimate sales price will obviously favor the seller. The size of these concessions should always be carefully studied to follow the trends in the negotiation.

It is easy to extrapolate the ultimate sales price by assuming that the same level of concessions will continue. If your client does not like where the extrapolation ends up, the party should alter the size of the concession to try to end up at a better ultimate sales price. Using a precise number when altering the pattern is even more powerful.

Major increases in the price being offered for a property and major decreases in the price the seller will take was much more common in the era where sellers built in plenty of room to reduce the sales price, and buyers started out at a very low price. The trend of the last decade has been to price properties for sale much closer to where they will ultimately trade because smart agents understand that a lengthy time on market generally begets a lower-than-market-value sales price. While there is still a focus on the relative size of monetary concessions by the buyer and seller, the trend in today's market is for margins to be smaller. This trend makes precise offers all that much more persuasive in a negotiation.

Chapter 33

THERE'S A LOT MORE TO NEGOTIATE THAN PRICE

WHILE MOST BUYERS and sellers focus on negotiating the sales price of the property, there is a lot more to negotiate than just price. Price is naturally one of the most important issues to both parties, but the other terms of the contract can have a huge impact on the ease with which the transaction is completed, the condition of the property at the time of closing, and the overall cost and timing of the transaction.

Among the other issues of importance include:

1. The date of closing

2. When possession of the property will transfer from seller to buyer

3. What repairs the seller makes

4. Who pays closing costs and transfer taxes

5. What fixtures and other property remains

6. Whether the purchase is conditioned on the appraised value of the property

7. Whether the purchase is all cash or conditioned on financing

8. Whether the purchase is contingent on the sale of other property

Timing is often the second most important issue to both buyers and sellers. The closing date and the date when possession of the property is transferred can make or break a deal. Sellers often need to be in a new house or city by a certain date and cannot close on their new home until their existing home has closed. Buyers often want to be in their new home before the start of school or some other major life event.

If a buyer cannot quite meet the seller's price but can meet the seller's other needs, the seller might very well be willing to take less. They might even pass up a higher-priced offer if the other terms on a lower offer are more appealing. Similarly, if the buyers have to pay more than they had hoped for a property, but the seller meets the buyer's other conditions, the buyer might be highly motivated to pay a higher price. The point is that it is often these finer points that determine whether or not the parties make it to the closing table. It is important not to allow yourself to become fixated on any one issue. If you encounter a sticking point during a negotiation, look for other issues that can help the parties bridge the gap.

These other issues will largely be irrelevant if the parties cannot get within striking distance of a deal based on price alone. But if they get close on price, conceding on one or more of these issues can make the difference in whether or not the parties reach an agreement. As a result, it is critically important for both agents to understand what else is important to the parties besides price. As we've previously explained, building a rapport with the other agent and picking up the telephone can help uncover these hot-button issues. We don't know what we don't know, and it is okay to ask.

Chapter 34

SAVE THE TOUGH STUFF FOR LAST

In NEGOTIATING, one goal should always be to get the other side totally invested in the negotiation. The longer parties negotiate with each other, the greater the likelihood they will reach some kind of resolution on the issues that separate them.

One way of doing this is to postpone the really tough issues that separate them for later in the negotiation after the parties reach an agreement on issues that can be more easily resolved. This is in keeping with the old proverb that "Life is simpler when you plow around a stump." Now, this does not mean that you can postpone basic issues like the price at which a property will be sold (although even this is occasionally done in some commercial transactions where the price is tied to a survey or an appraisal).

But if the parties are making progress on the basic issues in the transaction but there are some stumbling blocks that the parties just cannot seem to overcome, there is nothing wrong in saying, "Let's set that issue aside until the end and see if we can come to an agreement on the other issues."

People are generally much more willing to compromise on difficult issues when there is already a framework for an overall agreement. So, how do the remaining thorny issues get resolved? There are a few different ways that this can occur. First, the parties can trade concessions one for the other where each party gets their way on an issue until all issues are resolved. This is really no more than good old-fashioned horse trading where each party gives something and gets something.

Second, whether it is weariness or a sense that the parties are close and the end is in sight, people are more willing to compromise because they know that it will not open the door to negotiating over endless issues. Instead, making compromises brings the negotiations to an end. Therefore, it is important in trying to resolve the last few issues to reassure the other party that the resolution of these issues will truly be the end of the negotiation and that there will be no more "asks."

Chapter 35

SPEAK CONFIDENTLY, EVEN WHEN YOU ARE NOT FEELING CONFIDENT

GREAT NEGOTIATORS tend to exude confidence in their interactions with others. Whether it is a quiet confidence or confidence wrapped in brashness, successful negotiators have a certain swagger which silently communicates that they know what they are doing and can handle any situation that arises. When they negotiate, they speak with a sense of authority that tends to limit debate. For many agents, it takes years to develop this confidence.

If one does not have either the experience or the natural inclination to project confidence, how does one quickly develop this trait? The answer is to adopt an intense focus on projecting confidence and preparation. In other words, fake it until you make it!

Projecting confidence is about how you dress (professionally), walk into a room (in confident strides), shake someone's hand (firmly without squeezing), and how you look at them (in the eye without breaking the other person's gaze). And don't forget to do it all with a smile. Now, the above suggestions are for beginners. Once you have mastered that self-assured swagger, many of the above behaviors become automatic, and your reputation will precede you.

Developing confidence is also about preparation. Naturally, a less experienced agent is unlikely to know anywhere near as much as a seasoned agent. As a result, they must fill in what they lack in experience with studied knowledge about the specific transactions on which they are working. This does not mean that they need to become an expert on the entire body of knowledge affecting real estate brokers. That would likely be an impossible task anyway. Instead, they should learn everything there is to know about the property that they are helping to buy or sell and the neighborhood in which that property is located. If one becomes an expert at this micro level, they can usually hold their own with someone who is already an expert at a macro level.

Conveying confidence is also about the words you choose. Imagine how you would react as a listing agent if a buyer agent were to say to you with a very timid voice, "I know the seller has come down a lot on their price, but the buyer wanted me to ask if your client might consider one further price reduction to $640,000. The buyer really wants the house, but the price remains a bit out of their reach."

At the outset, this statement comes across like the agent doesn't believe in the reasonableness of the request and is being forced to ask it by the buyer. More importantly, it sounds like the buyer's agent does not want to lose the house and will meekly go away if told that no further price reductions are in the cards.

Some agents will go so far as to say, "It's okay if your sellers say no, but the buyers are making me ask if the sellers will reduce their price to $640,000." Here, the agent is not only disavowing any responsibility for the request, but they are also giving the seller's agent express permission to say no.

If you are afraid to ask a question, it should either not be asked or should be rephrased so you are comfortable asking it. Start by asking yourself why you are reluctant to ask the question. Usually, it is because as the agent, you think your own client is being unreasonable and is pushing too far. If that is the case, you should advise your own client not to keep pushing. But if your client insists, then figure out how to ask the question in a confident manner. At this point, your fear is that it will make you look foolish or unreasonable, elicit a strong negative response, and possibly kill the deal.

When considering how to speak confidently without eliciting a negative response, put yourself in the shoes of the listing agent. After going back and forth with offers and counteroffers and seemingly reaching a good middle ground, the last thing she is going to want is for the negotiations to continue. Therefore, it is important to clearly communicate that this is the final ask. She may still be frustrated that the negotiations are continuing, but at least the end will be in sight.

Additionally, never apologize for asking for a final concession or ask for it meekly. Instead, the request for a concession must be asked assertively as if you are sure it is going to be accepted. After all, the other agent really does not know the exact price at which a property will trade or the final terms that will be agreed to by the parties. The more confident you come across, the more the other agent may feel that whatever you are asking for really is reasonable.

A statement like the following conveys much more confidence: "I've got some good news. I've spoken with my buyer, and if the seller will reduce the sales price to $640,000, we have a deal." And, of course, if there is some justification for the request, that should clearly be articulated as well. Something like "The buyer has carefully studied the comps and believes that $640,000 is much more consistent with where the market is at this point."

Even if you follow this advice, the listing agent may still get annoyed or even angry that you've asked for an additional concession. If that happens, remain confident without arguing and do the following:

1. Acknowledge that you have heard the other agent by saying, "I hear what you're saying" or "I understand where you're coming from."

2. Do not say that you only asked because your client wanted you to do so. That sounds too much like you do not believe in the final request for a concession. Instead, endorse the client's position with "This seems like a reasonable ask to get the deal done."

3. Remind the other agent that this final concession will result in a deal. Something like "And when it is accepted by the sellers, we will be under contract and can move toward closing."

4. If the listing agent wants to continue to argue about the reasonableness of the request, avoid the argument with "I'm just trying to get the parties under contract. We present offers and counteroffers. Our clients then decide how to respond. We can both talk our clients out of a deal or make something happen here. As close as we are to a deal, it would be a shame for us to let this transaction fall apart."

This last statement introduces an element of uncertainty as to whether a deal will get done if the offer isn't accepted. Because agents are required to present all offers, it should end the discussion. If it does not, you can nicely remind the other agent that she has an obligation to present all offers and to please do so. Obviously, the success of this strategy will likely depend on the relative strength of the negotiating positions of the parties.

Now, put yourself in the role of the listing agent and consider how to respond when being presented with what you believe is an unreasonable request for

SPEAK CONFIDENTLY, EVEN WHEN YOU ARE NOT FEELING CONFIDENT

one final concession. Again, speaking from a position of confidence is the key. One way to do this is to warn the other agent of what you believe may be dire consequences if the offer is presented, and give the other agent the opportunity to rethink the wisdom of even making the final request for a concession. Something like the following might work: "I will, of course, present all offers and counteroffers. But as we both know, sometimes a transaction will completely fall apart when one side or the other pushes too far. I greatly worry that this will happen if I even present your request. Are you sure you want me to present it? You might consider going back and discussing the risks of my presenting what you have stated is your client's final counteroffer. If they still want me to present it and are willing to accept the risks, I will be glad to do so."

Such a statement can have a disconcerting effect on the other agent. You are telling them that they risk having the entire transaction fall apart if you even present their offer. You are asking them to get with their client and reconsider their approach. In some instances, the other agent will do so and accept your client's last offer without further negotiations. In either event, it is a good idea to share the communication with your client in a manner that will not inflame the situation.

In other instances, the agent will ask you to present the offer despite your warning. If that happens, it will be easier for your client to reject the offer. The key is to do so in a way that sounds like a minor victory for the buyer. A response like "Well, we still have an opportunity to save this transaction. The sellers did not pull the plug on the entire transaction although they did not accept your client's last offer. Hopefully, we can now bring these negotiations to a close and move forward based on my client's last counteroffer."

Chapter 36

THE CHALLENGES OF NEGOTIATING WITH YOUR CLIENT

AGENTS REPORT that some of the hardest negotiations they have are with their own clients. The biggest issues in such negotiations are (1) the length of the listing period or brokerage engagement and (2) the real estate commission that will be paid to the agent's broker. Put more succinctly from the perspective of the agent, how long are we going to work together and how much will I be paid?

Most clients understand the value of having an agent represent them as opposed to going it alone. Much has already been written about agents articulating their value proposition to prospective clients, and this book will not rehash the question of why clients should hire an agent.

Where the negotiations usually take place is over how agents should be compensated for their services. The good news is that many clients never question the amount of the agent's commission and simply accept whatever they are told is the going rate.

The clients wanting to negotiate with you over your commission tend to fall into three categories.

1. Those who want full service but at a bit of a discount

2. Those who want full service but at a limited service price

3. Those who want limited services at a limited service price

The arguments of the agent in response to client requests for a discount tend to be the following (or variations of these arguments):

1. I'm not a discount broker, and my commission is my commission.

2. I usually save my clients more money than the commission I am paid.

3. I only get paid if you sell or buy a house, and my commission reflects this risk.

4. You don't negotiate with your doctor or dentist; why are you negotiating with me?

5. You are buying or selling one of your biggest assets. Don't you want a capable agent professional by your side?

6. I wouldn't be much of a negotiator if I reduced my commission.

7. If I represent you in both the sale of your property and the purchase of another, I can give you a discount.

8. Do you know how little of the commission I actually get to keep?

The challenge with negotiating with a potential client is that these negotiations usually take place prior to your being hired. As a result, you have to negotiate in a way that still results in getting hired. In other words, you have to be exceptionally nice and avoid arguing.

What often seems to work best is to respond initially with a statement that does not invite discussion or negotiation. For example, if you say, "I hear what you are asking, but I do not negotiate my commission," it is a definitive statement that with most people ends further discussion. The potential client then either hires you or they don't.

With this approach, the agent has to accept that a small percentage of potential clients will not hire you. But, of course, this is a risk regardless of what you say to the potential client. The good news is that many clients do not interview multiple potential agents (even when they say that they are doing so). They interview one agent who they either know or was recommended to them with the thought that they will hire that person unless there is a reason not to do so. When the potential client is told that you don't negotiate your commission, many simply accept that this is the way it is with all good agents. Even if the potential client is interviewing other agents, you can still explain you don't negotiate your commission.

A less appealing alternative approach is to ask the potential client what kind of discount they are looking for. The potential client will often respond by suggesting a discount that is a percentage of the sales price. So, for example, let's say that the potential client asks for a discount of 1 percent of the sales price. The request is being asked in a way that makes it sound reasonable when, in fact, it is a significant reduction in your fees.

When this kind of request is made by a seller, it is normally best to ask if they want to reduce the commission to the buyer's agent and explain this may reduce the interest of buyer agents in showing the property. Most sellers want to maximize the likelihood of the sale taking place, so they may sheepishly ask that the discount be taken from the seller's side of the commission.

So, let's look at the following hypothetical where the listing agent quotes a 6 percent commission of the purchase price with 3 percent going to the buyer's agent. This leaves a 3 percent commission going to the seller's agent. If the 1 percent reduction being asked for by the seller all comes out of the listing broker's side, this means that the seller is asking you for a discount of one-third of your fee.

If the seller's agent asks the seller if they realize that they are asking the seller's broker to reduce the commission you earn as the listing agent by one-third, most are surprised and say that they did not realize they were asking for such a large commission reduction. If the listing agent also explains that out of the reduced commission the seller's agent pays for marketing expenses and that the agent's broker receives a portion of the commission (since, after all, the commission belongs to the broker), many sellers are reluctant to push for too large a commission reduction. Of course, by opening the door to the negotiation, there is often some commission reduction to which the parties agree. Therefore, the first approach discussed in this chapter of simply saying you do not negotiate your commission likely works better.

Negotiating with your own client after you are hired and during the real estate transaction is also very common and often difficult. Clients sometimes stop listening to your advice or surprise you by taking a completely unexpected position. The buyer or seller who gets cold feet and decides not to close is a prime example.

How do you get your own client centered again and back on track? There is a right way and a wrong way. The wrong way is to communicate through email, text, or telephone where the nuances of communication are often lost (as discussed in chapter 30). The right way is to meet face-to-face with your client where any issues of concern can be fully vetted.

Continuing with our example of the client who has decided not to go through with the transaction, you may want to start by asking her why and how she has reached this decision. Questions should be asked to get the client to explain their thought process in detail and confirm that all of the issues are out on the table.

The challenge is to get the client to rethink and change their position without making them feel like you are pressuring them to do so. Is this a negotiation? Yes, although it is a subtle one, but you should try not to make it feel like a negotiation. How do you do this?

After understanding the change of heart, our recommendation is to do three things:

1. See if there is a reasonable way to address whatever concerns the client may have.

2. Remind the buyer of the good things about the house and transaction and what they may be walking away from, and remind sellers about why they are moving in the first place.

3. Warn the client nicely of the adverse consequences of walking away from the transaction and suggest that they speak to an attorney before taking any action that could be considered a breach of the contract.

While the first two suggestions are easy enough to implement, the third one is the challenge. To the extent possible, the warning should be accomplished with questions that get the message across but do not do so in a threatening manner. So, instead of saying that the buyer will lose their earnest money or risk getting sued for a commission, you might ask, "Have you considered that you will lose your earnest money if you do not close?" or "Have you considered that you may owe the real estate commissions of the real estate brokers should you choose not to close?"

Discussing that the client may owe the commissions of both brokers can be put on personal or impersonal terms. An approach that helps keep the client on your side is to explain that your broker makes the decision as to whether or not to pursue a commission, not you, and it is not something that you control. If you want to make it personal, you can explain that you have worked very hard for the buyer and that the client deciding not to close hurts you financially in a very significant way.

Of course, while the nature of the warnings will vary depending on the state the broker is located in, there is a good likelihood that the client has not fully considered the consequences of her actions. If you again repeat the benefits of buying or selling the house, as the case may be, and encourage the client to reconsider their decision and speak to an attorney, they may do so. This is particularly the case if the client has not fully considered the legal consequences of her actions.

The key point here is that face-to-face meetings are the best way to work through difficult issues with your own client. You are typically not as constrained for time in person, can thoroughly discuss the consequences of the action the client is considering, and are more easily able to explore all solutions to the issues at hand.

Chapter 37

GET YOUR CLIENT TO PROPERLY PREPARE THE HOUSE

WHEN YOU THINK about the first thing most sellers do when they sell a car, it is almost always to get it detailed. Most people understand that newer-looking cars sell more quickly and for more money than older cars do, so spending the money to have a car detailed is a necessary and worthwhile expenditure. The same logic holds true in selling houses, but many sellers either do not have the money to spend to make the house look its best or they are not convinced that it will make a difference. After all, it is often far more expensive to prepare a home for sale than it is to prepare a car for sale. Some sellers also have blinders on when it comes to understanding that the condition or style of their home might deter buyers from making an offer.

Part of an agent's job is to convince the seller to spend the necessary time and money to get the property into showing condition. One easy way to do this is to repeat what our builder friends regularly tell us. New homes sell for about 30 percent more than used homes. The more your house does not look used, the higher the price you can normally get. This is done through decluttering, staging, and updating. Of course, with a stubborn seller, convincing them can be a chore. Fortunately, there are things that can help you.

First, depersonalize the advice. Create a presentation that contains a to-do list that all sellers should complete before listing a house. This can be a list that contains pointers such as putting away personal photos and removing small appliances, paper towel holders, and knife blocks from kitchen counters. The presentation can also contain general information about warm, neutral colors being more appealing to buyers, or statistics about time on market for properties that are properly staged.

The key is that you explain to your sellers that this is information you provide to all clients. It isn't a commentary on their cleanliness or style specifically. It is general advice for all. By generalizing the advice, a difficult pill becomes a bit easier for your seller to swallow. Taking the time to create a seller's guide that is professional, thorough, and helpful will not only be a tool to help you get your sellers to act but can also be a marketing tool that you use at listing presentations. "Hire me, and I'll provide you with a proven home-selling guide." You can therefore market yourself and the home.

Second, hire third-party professional consultants. Sometimes, a to-do list just will not do the trick for stubborn sellers. In those cases, bringing in a third-party consultant might be beneficial. Build relationships with stagers who will come into the home and consult with your seller about the best ways to get the home ready for showings. By hiring a third party, you can avoid being the one to have the difficult conversations. Additionally, having a neutral party tell a seller what needs to be done might be more convincing than if you alone suggest it. Sellers might be reluctant to pay for this sort of consultation, so having a relationship with the stager will likely help keep prices lower.

Third, be solution-oriented. It can be frustrating

when somebody tells you all of the things that are wrong with your house and then doesn't provide solutions. Say, for example, your seller has painted the inside of the house with vibrant, bold colors at a time when those are not in fashion. While appealing to the seller, they might be considered less appealing to buyers who do not have the vision to imagine themselves in the space. Recommending that a seller paint their house communicates the issue, but providing the seller with a list of three painters and arranging appointments for them to come give your seller a quote might help make an overwhelming project more manageable.

Regardless of whether or not your seller believes and is willing to make changes to prepare the home for showing, finding the money to get a house show-ready might still be an impediment. In those cases, try to figure out the changes that will make the biggest impact. Sometimes, just moving things around can create a big difference. Just like any negotiation in real estate, negotiating with a seller about preparing the home for sale can be challenging. Take the time to do your research and be thoughtful about your approach.

Most agents have imagination. If you are selling to

architects or interior designers, they have imagination as well. But the average buyer cannot see a house's potential. They only see what is right in front of them. Others see the potential but only want a house where everything has already been done. Either way, the agent needs to gently push their clients to make an investment in getting the house in show-ready condition in order to obtain the highest price possible.

Chapter 38

MARITAL DISPUTE RESOLUTION TECHNIQUES OFTEN WORK WELL IN NEGOTIATIONS

THIS IS GOING to sound like marital advice, but some negotiations are a little like having an argument with your spouse. In such disputes, there are four techniques that often work well both to resolve the marital dispute and help succeed in a negotiation.

The first is to acknowledge regularly and sincerely that you are hearing and understanding what the other agent is telling you. Agents know that in most negotiations, there will be compromises and neither party is likely to get everything they want. What is usually frustrating to all people is when a person feels they are not being heard (or understood) by the person with whom you are negotiating (or otherwise fighting with).

It is even appropriate to try to find some aspect of what the other person is saying with which you can state that you agree. This does not mean that you are surrendering your position. In most disputes and negotiations, there are always points of common agreement. What you are doing instead is looking to build a bridge with your counterpart in the negotiation and showing that you have respect for what they are saying. And, of course, while it does not mean that you cannot continue to advocate for your client's position, you can try to do it in a way where everyone feels good about the result.

The second technique is not to interrupt and let whoever you may be negotiating with completely finish their thought. Avoid asking "Are you done now?" as it can sound condescending like you have been humoring a child. This technique also has its roots in marital counseling. When we hear things with which we disagree, many of us are quick to want to jump into the conversation to correct what is being said. This tends to make the other person feel disrespected and that they have not been able to fully express themselves. Since most negotiations between agents are not done in person, one way to avoid interrupting is to grab a pad and write down counterpoints you want to make. This overcomes the primary reason people say they interrupt, which is that they are concerned they will forget something if they do not blurt it out right away. When the person is finished, it is always good to say something complimentary such as that you heard them (which, hopefully, you did) and they made several good points (which, hopefully, they did).

When it is then your turn to speak, try not to ever say that you disagree with what they have just said since doing so can sound needlessly confrontational. Instead, try to say something like your client has a different perspective on the situation, and here is how they view it. While this may sound a bit too diplomatic, thinking about how to keep from not sounding argumentative usually pays dividends.

The third recommendation is never to resort to name-calling or labeling what the other person is saying stupid, illogical, crazy, or anything similar. While that is certainly how you will feel from time to time, name-calling only pushes the parties further apart. As hard as it may be to do, particularly in the heat of a negotiation, the only way to make real progress is to explain your client's perspective on a given situation in hopes of finding compromise.

The fourth recommendation is to know when to take a break from the negotiation and reconvene at a later time. Sometimes, parties to a negotiation will reach an impasse that just cannot be overcome. When the parties are increasingly frustrated with one another, suggesting in a positive manner that they take a break can give everyone a chance to rethink their positions and possible solutions. Something like the following might be appropriate: "Look, I think we've accomplished a lot today. Let's stop for the day to give us both time to think about possible solutions to the remaining open issues. We both obviously want to work it out, and having some time to mull over the remaining issues might do us both good."

If the other party does not want to stop, you might say something like "You are obviously committed to wanting to resolve all issues immediately, which I greatly appreciate. I, for one, am tired and need to process the good progress we have made today and how we can resolve the issues that are left."

Before the parties break, it is often beneficial to make a list of what the parties have agreed to as well as the open issues that remain for when the parties reconvene. In this way, there is a guideline for how to efficiently address the remaining issues. It might also be helpful to set a specific time to continue the discussion.

Chapter 39

NEVER GLOAT IN WINNING A NEGOTIATION

THERE ARE WINNERS and losers in negotiations. Being a winner should mean that your client has achieved most of their goals. One rule for the winning party is to allow the losing party to save face to the extent that is possible and not mention that, in your opinion, they ended up on the short end of the stick in the negotiation.

There are two reasons for this. First, parties can always change their minds about selling or purchasing, including at the closing table. We have seen some boorish parties start to brag about the great deal they got at the closing table only to have the losing party walk out of the room and not complete the transaction. People have their pride and will be pushed only so far.

Second, one never really knows whether the other party has truly "lost" the negotiation or not. We once observed a seller brag at the closing table about how she sold her property for $50,000 over what comparable homes in the neighborhood had sold for. As soon as the closing papers were signed and the funds disbursed, the buyer mentioned that he had put together a land assemblage and already had the property he just bought under contract to be sold for three times what he paid for it. While this was arguably a win for both parties, the seller who had initially been bragging about her great win in the negotiation became stonily silent. Silence all the way around would have been a much better result.

It must always be remembered that the transaction is not over until the buyer and seller have closed, the seller has moved out, and the buyer has moved in. Even then, it is not really over until all statutes of limitations have run out on the buyer's ability to assert legal claims. Rub the buyer's nose into the reality that he was the loser in the negotiation and the buyer may just return the favor with a lawsuit later over the failure to disclose defects in the house. The reality is that the more positive the relationship between the parties, the less the likelihood that they will be fighting with each other later on. Also remember that you may have to work with the cooperating agent on a future transaction. If you brag about the great deal you negotiated for your client, you might make it more difficult to negotiate with that agent in the future.

Chapter 40

WEIRD THINGS BUYERS AND SELLERS DO IN NEGOTIATIONS

BUYERS AND SELLERS are known to respond in some weird ways in negotiations over buying and selling houses. While this could likely be a book in itself, here are a few of the more common peculiarities agents encounter.

1. Getting Caught Up in a Bidding War and Paying Far More for a Property Than They Should

Good auctioneers will tell you that their happiest moments in an auction are when multiple buyers get caught up in a bidding war. People's competitive spirit kicks in, and the price of the item being auctioned can get driven up beyond its fair market value. The same can be true in multiple-offer situations, particularly when they are fueled by the workings of an extreme seller's market.

Being the winner in a bidding war can initially create increased feelings of happiness, even if the buyer overpaid. It is a way for the winning bidder to show a spouse or partner that he or she is a take-charge problem solver who will step up to achieve a common goal of buying a particular house, even at a high price. It also just feels good to win.

One of the risks, however, is that the buyer may experience buyer's remorse either once they are under contract or after the closing. Sometimes the buyer, needing someone else to blame, may turn on the agent who, of course, should have protected the buyer from acting so rashly. In these situations, warning the buyer in advance and preferably in writing as they begin to get swept up in multiple offers is usually the best the agent can do to protect their clients and themselves. The message should be something like "While I know you really want this house, buyers in a bidding war tend to overpay. If the home doesn't appraise, you will likely have to pay the difference yourself. Are you sure you want to go down this road?" By clearly explaining the risks, you have increased the likelihood that the buyer will remain levelheaded.

The other option is to encourage your client to define the maximum price they would be willing to pay for the house and stick to it. What many buyers do in a bidding war is to focus on the wrong question, which is, "Am I willing to pay just an extra $20,000 (or whatever the extra amount is) to get a house I really want?" This gets the buyer focused on each incremental increase in the price of the house rather than on the fact that the buyer may be paying way above fair market value.

2. Becoming Unhappy If Their First Offer Is Accepted

There are many buyers who hate to negotiate and are thrilled if their first offer is accepted. There is also a group that interprets the acceptance of a first offer as evidence that they offered more money than they should have for a property. When representing buyers in this second group, there are two strategies to try to keep the transaction moving forward. The first is to explain to the buyer that there may well be a chance for further negotiations over repairs in which the buyer may benefit financially. The second is to point out that there are just as many people who hate negotiating as there are who love it, and the buyer may well be dealing with a seller who may have taken less than they wanted just to be finished with the negotiation.

For sellers considering accepting a first offer, you may want to advise them to counter in certain insignificant ways to avoid having the buyer end up feeling like she may have overpaid.

3. Losing a Deal Over a Couple Hundred Dollars

Some buyers and sellers view a negotiation as a pitched battle. They cannot accept what they perceive as losing a negotiation and see the process as a chance to display what they believe are their superior negotiation skills.

These are often the negotiators who push the negotiation to the absolute limit, take extreme positions, and at times refuse to make the small concessions needed to close out the negotiation. They are the ones who would often let a deal die rather than agree to a concession over a few hundred dollars.

How do you deal with such a party? There are two answers. First, as we discussed previously, try to keep them focused on the big picture of the transaction in which a few hundred dollars is almost always meaningless in the grand scheme.

Second, if the facts warrant it, compliment the person on what they have already achieved in the negotiation. Refusing to compromise over a few hundred dollars is almost always a matter of the person being prideful. They may see making the concession as essentially a loss of face. Reminding them of what they have objectively achieved in the negotiation is sometimes a way to bolster their spirits and encourage them to make the one final concession.

CONCLUSION

WHILE THE FOCUS of this book has been on how to become a better negotiator for people buying and selling real estate, it is really a book on how to become a better agent in general. The lessons of this book should help agents get more transactions closed with less difficulty.

What makes real estate negotiations so interesting is that there is an endless array of possible variations on what might happen in the course of a transaction. This book touches on the strategies and techniques that can be used in real estate negotiations. How they are applied and combined to the different negotiations you will see in the course of your real estate career is for each agent to discover.

Consciously thinking about these strategies and

techniques as you apply them to the different transactions with which you are involved, evaluating what worked and didn't work for you, and modifying your behavior to focus on what works is ultimately what will transform you into an excellent real estate negotiator.

ABOUT THE AUTHORS

SETH G. WEISSMAN is the senior partner in the law firm of Weissman PC in Atlanta, Georgia. He has been general counsel to the Georgia Association of REALTORS° for the last thirty years. Seth has always had a fascination with real estate negotiations and previously coauthored the book *Secrets of Winning the Real Estate Negotiation Game.* Seth has degrees from the University of Pennsylvania, the University of North Carolina at Chapel Hill, and Duke University.

KATHARINE B. OATES is a partner in the law firm of Weissman PC in Atlanta, Georgia, and a partner in several commercial real estate investment companies in Texas, Virginia, and Georgia. She has two decades of commercial and residential real estate experience working closely with developers, builders, investors, and agents. Katharine has degrees from the University of North Carolina at Chapel Hill and George Mason University School of Law.

Seth and Katharine are both actively involved in developing and teaching real estate negotiating seminars.